Nicholas Papadopulos has be
London, since January 2007. I
North End and was Senior C
for four years. Before ordina..... ... ,
is married to Heather Norton, a barrister and Recorder of the
Crown Court. They have two children.

GOD'S TRANSFORMING WORK

Celebrating ten years of
Common Worship

Edited by Nicholas Papadopulos

First published in Great Britain in 2011

Society for Promoting Christian Knowledge
36 Causton Street
London SW1P 4ST
www.spckpublishing.co.uk

British Library Cataloguing-in-Publication Data
A catalogue record for this book is available from the British Library

ISBN 978–0–281–06390–1

Typeset by Graphicraft Ltd, Hong Kong
First printed in Great Britain by Ashford Colour Press
Subsequently digitally printed in Great Britain

Produced on paper from sustainable forests

*For David Stancliffe,
Bishop of Salisbury 1993–2010,
Chairman of the Liturgical Commission
of the Church of England
1993–2006*

Contents

Contents

Contributors

Anders Bergquist is Vicar of St John's Wood Parish Church, London.

Jeremy Davies is Canon Precentor of Salisbury Cathedral.

Jeremy Fletcher is Vicar of Beverley Minster.

Richard Giles was Dean of Philadelphia from 1999 to 2008 and has now retired.

Peter Moger is Canon Precentor of York Minster.

Gilly Myers is Canon Precentor of Manchester Cathedral.

Nicholas Papadopulos is Vicar of St Peter's, Eaton Square, London.

Michael Perham is Bishop of Gloucester.

Simon Reynolds is Priest-in-Charge of Darton and Cawthorne, Wakefield.

Angela Tilby is Vicar of St Bene't's, Cambridge.

Rowan Williams is Archbishop of Canterbury.

Acknowledgements

The editor thanks Colin Podmore, David Hebblethwaite and Anthony Ball for their invaluable assistance in preparing this collection.

The publisher and editor acknowledge with thanks permission to reproduce extracts from the following. Every effort has been made to seek permission to use copyright material reproduced in this book. The publisher apologizes for those cases where permission might not have been sought and, if notified, will formally seek permission at the earliest opportunity.

Extracts from *Common Worship* are copyright © The Archbishops' Council, 2000, and are reproduced by permission. All rights reserved. <copyright@c-of-e.org.uk>

Common Worship: Christian Initiation is copyright © The Archbishops' Council, 2006, and extracts are reproduced by permission. All rights reserved. <copyright@c-of-e.org.uk>

Extracts from The Book of Common Prayer, the rights in which are vested in the Crown, are reproduced by permission of the Crown's Patentee, Cambridge University Press.

Extracts from *The Alternative Service Book 1980* are copyright © The Archbishops' Council, 1980, and are reproduced by permission.

Common Worship: Ordination Services, Study Edition is copyright © The Archbishops' Council, 2007, and extracts are reproduced by permission. All rights reserved. <copyright@c-of-e.org.uk>

Common Worship: Daily Prayer is copyright © The Archbishops' Council, 2005, and extracts are reproduced by permission. All rights reserved. <copyright@c-of-e.org.uk>

Stevie Smith, 'The Airy Christ'. Estate of James MacGibbon. Reproduced from The Collected Poems of Stevie Smith (Penguin Books/New Directions). By Stevie Smith, from COLLECTED POENS OF STEVIE SMITH, copyright © 1972 by Stevie Smith. Reprinted by permission of New Directions Publishing Corp.

Introduction
Common Worship, *common life:*
defining liturgy for today

ROWAN WILLIAMS

———————————◆◆◆———————————

One of the greatest gifts that Bishop David Stancliffe has brought to the liturgical life of the Church of England (and indeed much more broadly) has been his insistent reminder that thinking about liturgy obliges us to think about a great deal more than getting the words right. Getting the words right and leaving everything else to look after itself has been a perennial temptation for modern liturgical revisers in all the churches. But Bishop David has been clear that the words are less than half the task: liturgy happens in a particular space and it traces patterns within that space in a particular time. His own work, embracing music and architecture as well as the resonances of words and the exploration of the theology of the Church itself, has set standards for which the churches should be devoutly grateful. Yet, for all the energy that has gone into the formation of what we can call the *Common Worship* tradition and ethos in the Church of England, there are still some well-founded anxieties around. In what follows, I hope to offer some ways of clarifying what we mean by liturgy in a way that opens up some further theological dialogue within our Church; so that some of the indispensable insights embodied in the work of the last couple of decades, insights deeply shaped by David Stancliffe's thinking, can be brought out more sharply.

Is there a liturgical crisis in the Church of England? The language of crisis comes very easily to people's lips in these days, and I'm instinctively rather cautious about using it. At the same time, it would be a very eccentric and short-sighted

1

observer who would deny that in the Church of England at the moment, and doubtless in the Communion more widely, there is what could be described as a liturgical *drift*; a drift whose direction has the effect of increasing the distance between liturgy as traditionally understood, and the worship which seems to flourish in a good many of the larger congregations in our Church. It is a style of worship which is generally preferred by those in the Church who are involved in thinking about and taking forward 'Fresh Expressions' of ecclesial life. This distance finds its most obvious focus in specific questions about the use of robes, about the use of certain formulae, about a whole range of issues around the style of music, about posture and even the physical layout of worship spaces. But before we get too bogged down in that, it may be worth offering a little terminological clarification.

A great deal of worship in these newer contexts is in fact highly *ritualized*; but this doesn't necessarily mean that it is *liturgical*. It is of real importance to have some clear distinctions here. When we talk about *ritual* speech and behaviour, we are referring to rule-governed, habitual, repetitive and formulaic behaviour. And anybody who has ever experienced worship in supposedly modern church settings will be well aware that formulaic behaviour is by no means absent. There are contexts, indeed, where a not completely sympathetic observer might feel that the language and gesture used is as much a matter of codes for initiates as anything in the Book of Common Prayer or for that matter the Tridentine Missal. It is language and behaviour that takes for granted the insider's point of view, at least as much as more traditional forms do. It is unmistakably ritualized activity in the eyes of a detached observer; but what does it mean to say that it is not necessarily *liturgical* activity?

One emphasis that may be helpful in framing the rest of this discussion is to suggest that liturgy is an *event* in a physical space that has the effect of moving you from one context or condition of heart and imagination to another. Ritual doesn't necessarily have the effect of *moving* you in that way, shaping a journey into a new context; but liturgy is incomprehensible unless we think of it as in its essence involving a *transition*. As an event, it is something that does not leave you where you started. The paradox is that ritual behaviour isolated from this will always run the risk of leaving you in the same place; so that when we confront modern ritualized but unliturgical forms of worship, we are bound to ask what precisely is likely to be lost if one seems to be replacing the other, as well as asking the proper question of what bridges might be built between the different worlds involved.

I want to reflect on two dimensions of our humanity that are involved in liturgical activity, in the hope that this may sharpen up the distinction between that and mere ritual. Liturgy, we have suggested, is always something which effects a transition, an event of change. Liturgy transforms the self and its space. And this means that liturgy is bound to relate to two aspects of our human experience – our reality as *embodied* beings and our experience of ourselves as shaped through *time*. If we begin to understand a little better the sort of issues that are involved in reflecting on the body and time, we may get to a fuller sense of what effective liturgy must be. But to put it in those terms does at once focus for us why some of this is difficult at the moment – for the simple reason that we live in a culture which is often deeply illiterate about the body and uncomfortable with the passage of time.

It may seem strange to speak of illiteracy about the body in a culture which appears very interested indeed in material gratification of all kinds, and which is often described as materialist; and yet the notion that bodies are *organs of meaning* is not one that is easy to explain in our present context. This is the key difficulty – that we find difficulty thinking and experiencing the body as a signifying reality, a 'meaning' reality. Likewise we find difficulty in seeing and feeling the passage of time as meaningful; we are, very largely, trapped in *undifferentiated* time; we don't know how to *mark* time. But if these two things are true about the culture we're currently operating in, then liturgical activity, of the kind most of us are familiar with and most of us value, is this particular cultural moment proposing itself to an unprepared consciousness. I owe this way of putting it to an American philosopher of religion, Jacob Needleman, who argued many years ago in his provocative book, *Lost Christianity*,[1] that the trouble with Christian teaching like the Sermon on the Mount was that it was addressed to 'human beings who didn't yet exist'. That is, in order to hear exactly what the Sermon on the Mount is saying, you need to have arrived at a certain level of sheer human attentiveness and honesty. If we think about it, we can see that something of the same applies to liturgy in our age: a great deal of what we want to take for granted about liturgy is addressed to 'human beings who don't yet exist': it presents itself in an environment where it's almost impossible to translate what has traditionally been meant by 'the body' in liturgy and the use of time in liturgy.

Very often this is a problem that is wrongly diagnosed in our contemporary setting. It is not a matter of the language of liturgy being difficult and in need of being made easier, nor of the structure and visual tone of liturgy being alien and in need of being made familiar. Those are the tempting and easy mistakes that the 'kindergarten' liturgical reformer is most easily seduced by. It is worth underlining what I said earlier about some supposedly contemporary styles, which are in fact as alienating and impenetrable as any traditional forms to the uninitiated incomer. It is not simply a question of translating material from one medium or one idiom into another. We need a deeper recognition that there are dimensions of our current human cultural situation which make the whole notion of liturgy difficult. Crucially, of course, 'difficult' does not mean 'shouldn't be tried'. But this means that good liturgy, good liturgical reform or renewal, is obliged to think through these two themes of body and time rather more systematically than we have generally been used to. And it means also that we should not try to reduce this problem to the much less interesting problem – with its attendant temptations – of how you might translate something difficult into something easy.

The body communicates as a whole. It has certain organs which particularly (though not exclusively) focus the energy and reflection of human beings upon the business of communication: the noises we make have a very particular effect and, among the various physical motions for which we are responsible, are very specially flexible and creative. At the same time, we all know well enough what it is to listen to words coming from an expressionless face, and we know the great variety with which people accompany their speech in terms of gesture. The question posed by a schoolboy to an over-exuberant female schoolteacher – 'Miss, would you be able to talk if they cut off your arms?' – reminds us of just how varied that performance can be; and the work of contemporary neurologists has brought into focus more clearly than ever the interconnection of speech and gesture and the ways in which damage to limbs or other organs can literally impede spoken communication and understanding.[2]

The body communicates as a whole; but that also means of course that the body *receives* communication as a whole. That is to say that we don't just hear with our ears; we hear with all our senses. We absorb messages and process them through media far broader and more variegated than the ears alone. And this means that in this particular context we're bound to think of the liturgical event, the event of communication and transition, as an event which necessarily involves a whole environment, visual, aural and sensual. Significance is absorbed in all those ways and at all those levels. The language about the liturgy as 'heaven on earth' so often associated with the Orthodox liturgy may be overused (not to mention that in many contexts it may be wildly implausible and counter-intuitive ...), but it nonetheless relates to the absolute baseline of Christian identity, reflection and activity. It relates to the fact that liturgy is designed to be a transition into the new creation. And perhaps if we needed a single slogan to sum up the process of *Christian* liturgy, it should be 'movement into the new creation' – with all the implications that has for 'the liturgy *after* the liturgy', the outworking of the eucharistic and doxological experience in our daily discipleship; but that would need another essay or two.

It's a dimension of liturgy and of Christian identity that has been brought out more clearly than ever in the last few years by some unusual and innovative kinds of biblical scholarship. Unusual, because many of the assumptions of biblical scholarship in the last couple of generations have been based on the idea that essentially the Jewish world of Jesus' day was (to use a convenient and unfair British stereotype) rather 'low church' in style, approaching liturgy very much at the level of ideas and inspiration. But the work of writers like Margaret Barker[3] has stressed as never before how far the ritual of the Temple dominated the imagination of Jesus' contemporaries. Readers of Margaret Barker's work will find it difficult to approach the New Testament as once they might have done, because she demonstrates so vividly how the imagery, the metaphorical world, of Temple worship is pervasive in the New Testament; more specifically, she makes clear how that dimension of Temple ritual which was about re-establishing the order of the cosmos pervades much of the New Testament's thinking about the Christian life.

Jesus' Jewish world was a deeply liturgical world, a world in which the central activity for an entire culture and community was the cycle of annual events centred on the Temple, though not restricted to it, that had to do with the restoration of humanity to its proper place in creation. The divine image overlaid by the passage of time and the corruption of sin had to be laid bare and restored to its full glory. Humanity had to clothe itself afresh in the garments of light, lost at the beginning. In this process, humanity was revealed in its proper relationship to God and to creation as a whole. Liturgy in the Temple activated the buried divine image Godwards once again. And this was the language that was at hand for those early Christian believers seeking to make sense of the impact of the life and death and resurrection of Jesus. In the wake of these events, humanity had discovered itself afresh. It had been clothed anew in the garments of light, restored in its place before God and its relationship with the rest of the created order – and all because humanity had been invited, summoned to stand in the place of Jesus the New Adam, the Son of Man, the focus of God's creative and re-creative work and power.

So as the New Testament evolves and as its theology takes sharper and deeper form, part at least of what is going on is that the new Christian identity is being thought through and imagined in terms of that legacy of public performance of the narrative of humanity's history with God. The whole process of becoming a Christian and growing up as a Christian, growing as a believer into your full humanity as a believer, is to do with the same agenda that the Temple liturgy embodied. It is the celebration of the restoration of Adam to Adam's proper place in the cosmos. It is a clothing with light and (to use the opposite and complementary image) an uncovering of the naked likeness of God in human nature. So in terms of the entire environment in which liturgy takes place, the human body is receiving impressions with all its senses whose sole purpose is the restoration of the entire human being, spirit and body, in right relationship with God and the world. To reduce this to a matter of the exchange of ideas or the uttering of exhortations is to miss the deep and powerful current in Christian Scripture which is about new creation, restored relationship, even, to use the more formidable term, an 'ontological' change of location and identity. And at this level of course, it connects with questions around time.

Liturgy is an event of transition; something changes; where you are at the end is not where you were at the beginning; and, if the earlier parts of this discussion were along the right lines, understanding liturgy properly is understanding the specific changes and movements which this or that liturgical act involves. So liturgy is itself a temporal activity, it takes time – and it takes 'differentiated' time. Differentiated time is the opposite of the unmarked time of the seven-day working week; the opposite of time without rhythm; the opposite of time considered simply as a medium you can use in order to make money, to make yourself secure, to guarantee profit or whatever.

The more time is seen simply as the opportunity for such ego-directed activity, the less differentiation there is. It is much better (we seem to assume) to have seven working days without a break than to have these tiresome interruptions all the time where for 24 hours you can't actually make profit to justify your existence. You do not have to be a dedicated, old-style sabbatarian to feel that the Sabbath principle is a precious one – expressed, of course, most wonderfully in the liturgies of the Jewish Sabbath eve meal with Jewish friends, which crystallize the idea of a day that is to be encountered as sheer gift and grace, to be welcomed like a bride.

But this is deeply counter-cultural at the moment. Global communication and the global economy, and the work patterns already referred to, all of this pushes us in the direction of a time that is flattened out – sheer duration, without shape or rhythm, what I called earlier *unmarked* time. This is, more and more, the kind of time in which we are encouraged – and sometimes obliged – to live. In contrast, liturgical time is the opposite of time that just has to be filled up. It is the time of a drama, the time of an event. It is thus to do with the building and release of tension, and the time needed for transition to happen. It is differentiated time, time that has a 'shape' to it and as such it casts a different light on how we spend the rest of our time (or at least it should). The element just noted of building and releasing tension is, again, something which we are very easily seduced into losing sight of in liturgy. And it is this which most clearly marks the difference between ritual and liturgy. The worship event which has no story to tell and no rhythm to follow may be highly ritualized, but what it is not is liturgical, that is, transformative. It may have its own virtues and its own strengths, but they're not specifically liturgical.

It was Helen Gardner who many years ago in her work on religion and literature[4] noted the differences between Eastern and Western liturgy, saying that, whereas Western liturgy was 'romantic', Eastern liturgy was 'epic'. She did not, of course, just mean the obvious thing about the length of Eastern liturgy, but was observing that Western liturgy was far more dominated than Eastern by the processes of building and releasing tension. The Western liturgy moved towards a single, dramatic, climactic moment and released that tension; Eastern liturgy is less defined by a movement towards *one* culminating point. And although I believe she underrates the dramatic and 'romantic' qualities of Eastern liturgy, it is an argument that obliges us to think about the nature of the building and releasing of tension as a necessary aspect of liturgy which takes time and has dramatic energy, in the broadest possible sense.

And so in a culture where this approach to time seems increasingly strange, or eccentric, the good liturgical act becomes yet again a very counter-cultural moment. It poses questions about our use and understanding of time, and conversely it makes liturgy itself *difficult* in a potentially very creative sense. In our undifferentiated time of modernity, it may seem to many fairly obvious that an hour spent in worship doesn't have to have much of a shape and doesn't have to have much of a story to it. But the liturgist should be challenging this in the name of a fundamental recognition, rooted in the world of Jesus himself, that the point of standing before God is to move into the new creation with its new possibilities and its new obligations. A great deal more could be and has been said on these matters of understanding the body, the entire material environment, and understanding time, rhythm, and tension. These are what constitute the *story* of the liturgical event. But the main point here is to outline some of the underlying cultural issues that we often fail to look at adequately as we think about liturgy these days – whether or not we have a 'liturgical crisis' in the Church of England or anywhere else.

Rather than simply opposing traditional liturgy and contemporary worship, we need to look at where the bridges might be built and where the challenges specifically are. Thus I believe it is right to ask, in the context of the typical contemporary worship service: How much education is going on about what Christianity takes for granted about the body and the world? This is because I believe that in introducing people afresh to the Christian faith, we have to bear in mind that this faith is not simply the acquisition of some new ideas or even of some new emotions. It is moving into a set of renewed relationships with God and the world, moving into the new creation – and so understanding that the ambient world is not what we thought it was. In dealing with a congregation of people coming from our contemporary culture with very little preparation for or grasp of this, there is an enormous opportunity for laying out the fact that Christianity actually gives you a way of existing as a material being in the world that was not there before. It is an area where we can take a lesson from our Buddhist friends for whom the practice of faith is fundamentally a different way of being a material creature in the world. It may be objected that this is by no means what Christian faith in its fullness means, and I would agree; but without something of this material or bodily 'wisdom' about how we understand ourselves and behave ourselves as material beings, invitations to faith continue to be addressed to 'people who do not yet exist'. We readily lose sight of this in the Western religious world, and we need to recover such a perspective with some intelligence and imagination.

How, then, does the very exciting and invigorating new world of outreach bring into its purview the essential question: What kind of *material world* does Christian faith bring you into? This is where we need to grasp a little more fully what faith entails about the passage of time and the use of time. And second, coming out of that, there is the question: How can traditional liturgy, in the broadest sense of those words, emerge from such questions as something that is not simply weird or eccentric but genuinely about new perception and sensation?

The traditional forms of liturgy take for granted certain things about the body and time; and to be able to present those insights and those assumptions coherently as part of what the liturgical event is about has to be among the main challenges for theorists and practitioners of liturgy in our own difficult times. Very often the stand-off (as it sometimes seems) between traditional liturgy and modern ritual is misconceived. The traditional is valued simply because of its archaic or even picturesque quality rather than because of its substantive theological depth. If certain styles of worship and certain bodily postures and gestures matter, it is not simply because they've been done since the days of the apostles (or since the days of the vicar before last); they matter because they say something about the new humanity within the new creation. How do we communicate that? Not simply by repetition but by entering into the depth of those things, as wisdom and as discipline. It needs a great deal of discernment. There are, as we all know, attitudes to traditional liturgy which are defensive, unintelligent or even superstitious. But there are a good many cases where (a little reluctantly perhaps) we've come round to realizing that what thirty years ago might have seemed a pointless refinement, and therefore dispensable, actually enabled a quality of bodily concentration which we wouldn't otherwise experience in our liturgy, so that losing this has meant that some significant dimension of liturgy's essence has been forgotten.

This, of course, as I hinted at the start of this essay, opens up a whole set of fascinating, difficult questions which can't be addressed here, questions to do with the architecture of the space in which this transition happens, and the right and the wrong levels of flexibility in that physical space. These are subjects for ongoing discussion. But what I am concerned to underline is that the service given to the Church of the future by committed liturgists and liturgiologists is not simply about liturgical scholarship in its narrower sense, but about the revitalization of that liturgical theology which understands liturgy as the transformation of the time-taking body within the material world. For very many, the work of somebody like the late Fr Alexander Schmemann as a liturgical theologian has been transformative in this area in approaching the event of Christian liturgy with a deep concern for liturgy as a dimension of Christian identity, an experience of new creation, the renewal of soul and body, and the re-balancing of the whole created order in Jesus Christ.[5] The task before us is moving into the theological depths of the liturgical action on the basis of an understanding of what the liturgical *transformation* is.

It is a challenge, of course, for our whole Church, not only for liturgical specialists. Part of my own concern about the situation regarding liturgy in our Church is not so much about the disappearance of this or that text from education and practice or about shifts in style; it is a more pervasive worry about whether we have discovered how to educate clergy and laity in behaving liturgically – by which of course I *don't* mean the angle at which you hold your thumbs. Learning liturgical behaviour is learning to *use your body significantly*. A great many people emerge from our training institutions with very little sense of what that might mean, or of how the use of the celebrant's body enables or disables the whole community's worship. But no theological student is going to grasp that without some theology to underpin it.

So, is there a liturgical crisis? There is in many areas probably better practice in liturgy than there's been for quite a long time, thanks to an imaginative Liturgical Commission and the initiative (more short-lived than some would like) of national resourcing for liturgical development and education. And there is also a great deal that is worse. I hesitate simply to use the word 'crisis'; but I should want to identify an *opportunity* and, above all, a *challenge* in what I believe is a profoundly exciting dimension of our theology and our understanding of what it is to be a Christian. Because if any of this is along the right lines, then understanding our liturgy is understanding our *newness* as Christians: understanding what difference is made by the death and resurrection of Jesus. The heart of *all* our liturgical activity is, and should always be, Paschal. The event of liturgy is always the one event on which the history of our world turns; and liturgy that is alive and makes faith alive in us is liturgy that engages with the endlessly exciting calling to realize the one Paschal mystery in the incalculable variety of human cultures and languages – even the curiously amnesiac and driven culture in which we are now called to celebrate the Risen Lord and his gift of renewal.

Notes

1 Jacob Needleman, *Lost Christianity: A Journey of Rediscovery to the Center of Christian Experience*, New York, Doubleday, 1980, especially ch. 8.
2 See for example the groundbreaking work of Iain McGilchrist, *The Master and His Emissary: The Divided Brain and the Making of the Western World*, New Haven and London, Yale University Press, 2009, particularly, on this subject, pp. 66–77 and the whole of ch. 4 for the broader context of sense-making in and through the two cranial hemispheres.
3 See particularly Margaret Barker, *The Great High Priest*, London, T&T Clark, 2003, and *Temple Themes in Christian Worship*, London and New York, T&T Clark, 2007.
4 Helen Gardner, *Religion and Literature*, London, Faber and Faber, 1971, pp. 114–15.
5 See particularly Alexander Schmemann, *Introduction to Liturgical Theology*, Crestwood, NY, St Vladimir's Seminary Press, 1966, and *For the Life of the World*, Crestwood, NY, St Vladimir's Seminary Press, 1972.

Part 1

COMMON WORSHIP: CONSIDERING THE LITURGY

1

The silent music of our praise

Michael Perham

Ten years on from the authorization of *The Alternative Service Book* (*ASB*) of 1980 the pressure had begun for the revision of the rite and to add to its Eucharistic Prayers. That there is no similar pressure in relation to the *Common Worship* eucharistic rites (save in relation to Eucharistic Prayers when children are present) ten years after the revision of 2000 bears witness to the fact that the current rites have been an enrichment of what has gone before and are satisfying the need in the Church for good liturgy that enables the people of God to draw close to God in worship.

It is profitable to explore why that may be. At least three answers suggest themselves. One is the literary quality and richer theological imagery of much of the new material, notably within the Eucharistic Prayers. Another is the clarity of shape and structure in the rite. A third is, perhaps, a turning of the tide where people have ceased to yearn for endless variety and have recognized the value of repetition and memorability in worship. This chapter explores all three, as well as noting some other features of the way that Holy Communion Order One has been received and assimilated in the life of the Church of England.

One important difference between the ways the 1980 and 2000 liturgies have been received is in the way the texts have been presented to congregations. In 1980 many churches (parishes and chaplaincies) purchased full sets of the large brick-like *ASB* and issued these to congregations to use in worship. It seemed a welcome return to the old days where people had used the Book of Common Prayer, often bringing their own copy to church with them. It marked the end of a decade or more of living with liturgy in pamphlets. But the reality was that the book was too large to handle and the rite too complex to follow and, besides that, the era of the pamphlet had changed what people found helpful. Other churches used the slim red 'separate', which avoided the large book, but retained the complexity of the rite. Gradually, especially with the development of desktop publishing, parishes began to create their own versions, particularly in the interest of making the service more accessible to visitors and newcomers.

In the year 2010 very few churches choose to use a large book or a 'separate' from Church House Publishing. The local version has become the norm. In terms of good and vibrant liturgy this has been a mixed blessing. Some churches have produced their own version that excludes all variety. There is a whole deanery in the north of England that has used for ten years a form that makes the use of seasonal material unlikely and prints only one Eucharistic Prayer. It is Prayer A, one of those almost unaltered from the 1980 book and the 1971 Series 3 that preceded it. Such local versions exist in many churches, making the rite almost as inflexible as the Book of Common Prayer and depriving the congregation of most of the richness that will be described in this chapter.

However, in the majority of churches, the local version, or, more likely, the collection of local seasonal versions, has made the liturgy more flexible, easier to follow and richer in liturgical and theological content. This has been the more so where those designing the booklets have resisted the temptation to include too much text. In *Common Worship* the Liturgical Commission attempted to discourage people from focusing on the written word at the expense of the liturgical action by printing the full text of the Eucharistic Prayers not in the main order of service, but in the supplementary material, instead giving the congregation in the main text only the words they needed to respond to the presidential texts. But there is in many churches a desire to have the full text. Once it is provided, it is more difficult for the leader of worship to introduce variety and spontaneity to match the occasion.

Before turning to the Eucharistic Prayers, it is worth exploring how successful have been the attempts to move the celebration on from the norms of the 1980s and 1990s. In terms of clarity of shape, the clear fourfold pattern of the eucharistic liturgy has established itself. The Gathering leads into the Liturgy of the Word, the Liturgy of the Word into the Liturgy of the Sacrament, the Liturgy of the Sacrament into the Dismissal, though it is a pity that the order for the Eucharist did not follow the Initiation Services in naming the final section 'The Sending Out', which has a more dynamic imperative to it. Within the rite, the placing of the penitential material at one place, as part of the Gathering, rather than, as in 1980, printing it twice with a choice to use it as part of the preparation or in response to the Liturgy of the Word, has brought clarity and established a norm. In general a greater care about notes and rubrics has helped those leading and participating to understand more clearly the flow of the liturgy. One particular example of this, though one that is still ignored in a number of churches, is the clear instruction to precede the Collect with an invitation to silent prayer, so that the Collect recovers its traditional role as the collecting up of the prayers of the whole community, rather than becoming a theme prayer, setting the scene for the readings, as it had become in 1980.

In terms of richer language, often expressing more engaging theology, there is reason to be grateful that a number of evocative texts are now in the main order, rather than hidden in supplementary material where many people failed to find them. Among the texts that have now become part of the repertoire of many congregations are the alternative form of confession ('Most merciful God, Father of our Lord Jesus Christ, we confess . . .'), originally part of the 1970 revision of Morning and Evening Prayer, with its satisfying lines that draw on Micah 6.8:

> In your mercy
> forgive what we have been,
> help us to amend what we are,
> and direct what we shall be;

that we may do justly,
love mercy,
and walk humbly with you, our God.[1]

There are also the alternative invitations before the distribution, the first, rich in Scripture, drawing on the Roman rite,
and incorporating phrases from Matthew 8.8, John 1.29 and
Revelation 19.9.

> Jesus is the Lamb of God
> who takes away the sin of the world.
> Blessed are those who are called to his supper.
> **Lord, I am not worthy to receive you,**
> **but only say the word, and I shall be healed.**
> (Invitation to Communion,
> Holy Communion, Order One)

The second, which comes from the Eastern Church and dates
back to the fourth century, is based on 1 Corinthians 5.7–8.

> God's holy gifts
> for God's holy people.
> **Jesus Christ is holy,**
> **Jesus Christ is Lord,**
> **to the glory of God the Father.**
> (Invitation to Communion)

Both these theologically rich texts existed in the supplementary material of the 1980 rite, but neither were in frequent
use until brought into the main order in 2000. Particularly in
the case of the 'Jesus is the Lamb of God' text, it is an example,
of which there are others, of a text that had previously seemed
to be associated with a particular churchmanship (in this case
Catholic), being brought into the mainstream and used by people
of widely different traditions.

Another example of that phenomenon is the use of the
Roman offertory prayers, slightly changed to meet Evangelical
sensitivities about 'offering'. In this case the texts have not been
brought into the main text, though the response 'Blessed be
God for ever' has been and, with the printing of local versions,
this dual text has become firmly established in many places,

though not to the exclusion of some other particularly well crafted 'prayers at the preparation of the table'.

David Frost's fine alternative version of the so-called 'prayer of humble access' has also become better known for its inclusion in the main order.

> Most merciful Lord,
> your love compels us to come in.
> Our hands were unclean,
> our hearts were unprepared;
> we were not fit
> even to eat the crumbs from under your table.
> But you, Lord, are the God of our salvation,
> and share your bread with sinners.
> So cleanse and feed us
> with the precious body and blood of your Son,
> that he may live in us and we in him;
> and that we, with the whole company of Christ,
> may sit and eat in your kingdom.
>
> > (Prayer before the distribution,
> > Holy Communion, Order One)

It was written, as a contemporary equivalent to Thomas Cranmer's original, for Holy Communion Series 3, alongside his Post-Communion Prayer, 'Father of all, we give you thanks and praise', but the General Synod judged that the Church would prefer to stay with the traditional prayer and Frost's version was rejected, reappearing in 1980 in the supplementary texts. His Post-Communion Prayer, written originally as a presidential text, has been found to work as a congregational prayer, and is such in the 2000 rite and, because it is spoken together by the whole worshipping community, its richness in theological themes has become part of their understanding of Christian faith.

The 2000 rite has also acquired a stronger Trinitarian emphasis, giving a liturgical encouragement to the recent recovery of Trinitarian theology after a period of neglect, a recovery that is reinforced by the return in the 2000 calendar to 'Sundays after Trinity' once Eastertide is over. The Gathering may begin with 'In the name of the Father . . .', and the Collect conclude with the

Trinitarian ending, and the default text to introduce the prayers of intercession is 'In the power of the Spirit and in union with Christ, let us pray to the Father'. Among a collection of prayers after communion in the supplementary material is this fine Trinitarian prayer from the Scottish *Book of Common Order*.

> You have opened to us the Scriptures, O Christ,
> and you have made yourself known in the
>   breaking of the bread.
> Abide with us, we pray,
> that, blessed by your royal presence,
> we may walk with you
> all the days of our life,
> and at its end behold you
> in the glory of the eternal Trinity,
> one God for ever and ever.
>
> (Supplementary Texts:
> Prayers after Communion)

Its more frequent use would further strengthen the Trinitarian nature of the Eucharist, which is at its strongest in the Eucharistic Prayer itself, when, in a variety of texts, the Church asks the Father to send the Spirit to make the bread for us the body of the Son.

The emphasis on the Trinity is at its strongest, of course, on Trinity Sunday, when there is a set of texts specifically for that feast. It is one of 15 such sets, one for every season and for every principal holy day except Good Friday. For each there is an invitation to confession, a Gospel acclamation, an introduction to the Peace, eucharistic Prefaces and a blessing. The intention, and it has been well fulfilled in many churches, is that there shall be variety across the year, but consistency through a season. By their use for a number of weeks, the seasonal texts, most of which are biblical, begin by repetition to enter the memory. The building up of a memory bank, after some years, of such variety that people have a few texts they can remember and which can feed their soul, is a significant gain.

Among those 15 new texts are the 15 Gospel acclamations, which, other than in Lent, are Scripture verses enveloped in alleluias. Here is another significant enrichment of the eucharistic liturgy – heralding the Gospel with alleluias – and its use has become widespread: sometimes spoken, which is a start, sometimes sung, which is better, whether to the traditional chant or to a more contemporary tune.

All these elements have brought both depth and colour to the celebration of the Eucharist in the last ten years. But they have not been as significant for the renewal of worship as the Eucharistic Prayers that are part of Holy Communion Order One and it is to these that we now turn.

It is worth recalling a little twentieth-century history. Holy Communion Series 1, authorized from 1966, made legal a number of liturgical practices that had established themselves in the earlier decades of the century and included a Eucharistic Prayer that brought together the 1662 Prayers of Consecration and Oblation, retaining the Prayer Book language, though by joining the two prayers together departing both from its liturgical shape and its theology. Holy Communion Series 2, published in 1966 and authorized a year later, the first entirely new authorized eucharistic rite in the Church of England since 1662, adopted the classical shape of the Eucharist and of the Eucharistic Prayer, from which the Prayer Book had departed. Its one Eucharistic Prayer was stark and simple, beautiful but spare, the language a compromise between Cranmer's Tudor English and contemporary language – 'thee' and 'thou' were retained. Five years later, in Series 3 the Church of England had its first contemporary-language eucharistic liturgy. The Eucharistic Prayer, though identical in shape to Series 2 and judged by most to be theologically similar, was an entirely new text. Again there was one prayer, with the only variety being in a number of short 'proper Prefaces'. The rite of 1980 made a major change in increasing the number of Eucharistic Prayers to four, allowing choice for the first time. Prayer 1 was that from Series 3. Prayer 2 was a modern translation, with a few new lines, of the Series 2 rite. Prayer 3 was, for Anglicans, entirely new, based on the third-century liturgy of Hippolytus, and with some resonances of one of the Roman Catholic Eucharistic Prayers, based on the same source. Prayer 4 was basically that of Series 1, the Prayer Book text, but modernized, with the classical shape. During the 20 years of the authorization of the *ASB*, Prayer 1 was the most used, presumably because it represented simple continuity with Series 3 that most churches had used through the 1970s, and Prayer 3 established itself alongside it. Prayer 2 was used rather less, Prayer 4, with its Prayer Book style and theology, rarely (in many churches not at all). There was a variant on Prayer 4, still in modern English but with the Prayer Book shape, the prayer ending with the words of institution. This was designed for a small conservative Evangelical constituency, which did indeed use it.

That is the background to the Eucharistic Prayers of *Common Worship*. The Liturgical Commission proposed six for the 2000 rite. The General Synod added two more. Of the 1980 prayers, Prayer 1 re-emerged, amended, as Prayer A, 3 as B and 4 as C. Prayer 2 disappeared, though a few key phrases reappeared elsewhere, and five new prayers were authorized. Prayer E was newly composed within the Liturgical Commission, following the same Western pattern of prayer as A, B and C, but with a lighter narrative style. In particular it includes a very short Preface before the Sanctus that can be replaced by one of the many extended Prefaces for seasons and feasts.

Prayers F and G broke new ground in a number of ways. Prayer F is based on the Liturgy of St Basil, which may go back as early as the fourth century, and is still sometimes used in the Eastern Church. It has also formed the basis of Eucharistic Prayers in The Episcopal Church (TEC) and in the Roman Catholic Church. Prayer G, one of the two introduced into the General Synod during the revision process, began life as the fruit of work in the Roman Catholic Commission on English in the Liturgy, but which had never been authorized. These two prayers, though different from one another, have three significant factors in common.

The first is the position of the *epiclesis*, the invocation of the Spirit upon both the gifts and the people. Space here does not allow a detailed discussion of what has been in the past a hotly debated issue, but, to express it simply, the Western tradition has tended to have a double *epiclesis*, calling down the Spirit first on the bread and wine before the words of institution, those words frequently being regarded as 'consecratory', and then calling down the Spirit on the community later in the prayer. That pattern is explicit in Prayers A, B and E. In the East, the *epiclesis*, rather than the words of institution, has been understood as the key text for 'consecration', and this *epiclesis* has been a single one, seeking the Spirit's transformation of the gifts and the people, towards the end of the prayer. Prayers F and G both opt for the single late *epiclesis*. In Prayer F it reads

> As we recall the one, perfect sacrifice of our redemption,
> Father, by your Holy Spirit let these gifts of your creation
> be to us the body and blood of our Lord Jesus Christ;
> form us into the likeness of Christ
> and make us a perfect offering in your sight.
> (Holy Communion, Order One, Eucharistic Prayer F)

The equivalent in Prayer G is

> Pour out your Holy Spirit as we bring before you
> these gifts of your creation;
> may they be for us the body and blood of your dear Son.
>
> As we eat and drink these holy things in your presence,
> form us in the likeness of Christ,
> and build us into a living temple to your glory.

Although there are some in the Church of England who will not use these prayers because they do not conform to the Western pattern used by the Roman Catholic Church, their acceptance has been general and Prayer G is one of the most frequently used prayers. This represents a change from an earlier period when the proposed Prayer Book of 1928 was rejected partly because of the unacceptability then of the Eastern shape that its eucharistic rite embraced. The advance it represents, of course, is to articulate a clearer theology of how the Holy Spirit transforms the elements as part of the same action as the renewal of the people. In being renewed as the body of Christ the Church receives the body of Christ.

The second common element in these two prayers is the introduction of an intercessory element. They are the only two prayers in which this provision is made. Prayer F prays

> Look with favour on your people
> and in your mercy hear the cry of our hearts.
> Bless the earth,
> heal the sick,
> let the oppressed go free
> and fill your Church with power from on high.

In Prayer G, a brief intercessory text leads into an opportunity for interpolation or even for spontaneity.

> Remember, Lord, your Church in every land.
> Reveal her unity, guard her faith,
> and preserve her in peace ...

In Thomas Cranmer's first Prayer Book of 1549, intercession formed part of the Prayer of Consecration, but in subsequent Anglican rites it had been suppressed, because of the fear that intercession within the Eucharistic Prayer would suggest a sense of 'offering the mass' for an intention in a way unacceptable in the reformed tradition. Its return, now that such fears seem unfounded, is welcome, though it needs to be stated that there is little evidence of clergy developing the confidence to add to the text in a way that they are invited to do. There is room here for a greater grasping of the freedom offered.

The third element is the richness of the imagery in these two prayers. It is difficult to isolate particular phrases and sentences, for the effect of the more evocative phraseology is cumulative. But sentences like these come immediately to mind:

> for by the breath of your mouth
> you have spoken your word,
> and all things have come into being.   (Prayer F)

> You fashioned us in your image
> and placed us in the garden of your delight.   (Prayer F)

Lord God, you are the most holy one,
enthroned in splendour and light.   (Prayer F)

Embracing our humanity,
Jesus showed us the way of salvation;
loving us to the end,
he gave himself to death for us;
dying for his own,
he set us free from the bonds of sin,
that we might rise and reign with him in glory.
                                                      (Prayer F)

From the beginning you have created all things
and all your works echo the silent music of your praise.
In the fullness of time you made us in your image,
the crown of all creation.   (Prayer G)

How wonderful the work of your hands, O Lord.
As a mother tenderly gathers her children,
you embraced a people as your own.
When they turned away and rebelled
your love remained steadfast.

From them you raised up Jesus our Saviour, born of Mary,
to be the living bread,
in whom all our hungers are satisfied.

He offered his life for sinners,
and with a love stronger than death
he opened wide his arms on the cross.   (Prayer G)

By 2000 the Church of England was ready for poetic language
such as this. In the decades before there had been a conscious
move away from the literary beauty of the Prayer Book tradition and a desire for words in worship that were stark, terse
and direct. In some ways this matched the prevailing culture
in art and in architecture. But after a while this simplicity began
to wear thin, and indeed some were never enamoured of it and
longed for the resonance of the Prayer Book. The literary and
theological richness of these prayers meets that need. Both these
prayers, perhaps Prayer G rather more than F, have established

themselves in frequent use. The consequence, happily, is the feeding of souls with vivid and memorable phrases that nourish not only when sharing in the liturgy, but whenever those who know them reflect on their faith and spirituality.

There is an important question that needs to be asked. It is one thing to make the language of liturgy richer. It is quite another to move the theological goalposts, especially in a church that insists so clearly that its liturgy is where you find its doctrine. Eloquent as they are, the sentences quoted above do not represent a new emphasis, let alone a change, in doctrine. They simply clothe the gospel in fresh words and phrases. But there are two areas where the emphasis in the new prayers seem to give a new signal.

The first is in what they say about the Eucharist itself and the death of Jesus. This has been an area of sensitivity through-out Anglican history and, in the revisions of the late twentieth century, there was much debate about exactly how to express this relationship and how to employ the language of sacrifice. The prayers that existed before 2000 spoke in these ways:

> we remember his offering of himself
> made once for all upon the cross
> . . .
> we make the memorial of Christ your Son our Lord.
> . . .
> Accept through him, our great high priest,
> this our sacrifice of thanks and praise
> > (Holy Communion, Order One,
> > Eucharistic Prayer A)

> . . . calling to mind his death on the cross,
> his perfect sacrifice made once for the sins of
>   the whole world;
> . . .
> we celebrate this memorial of our redemption.
> As we offer you this our sacrifice of praise and
>   thanksgiving,
> we bring before you this bread and this cup
> > (Prayer B)

> in remembrance of the precious death and passion,
> the mighty resurrection and glorious ascension
> of your dear Son Jesus Christ,
> we offer you through him our sacrifice of praise
> and thanksgiving.   (Prayer C)

Despite their variety at other points, when it comes to the *anamnesis*, these prayers are remarkably uniform in their language – making and celebrating a memorial, offering a sacrifice of praise and thanksgiving. So it is striking that some new phrases occur in the prayers that were first authorized in 2000.

> . . . with this bread and this cup
> we celebrate the cross
> on which he died to set us free.
> Defying death he rose again
> and is alive with you to plead for us and all the world.
>   (Prayer D)

> . . . we remember all that Jesus did,
> in him we plead with confidence his sacrifice
>   made once for all upon the cross.

> Bringing before you the bread of life and cup of salvation,
> we proclaim his death and resurrection
> until he comes in glory.   (Prayer E)

> . . . we proclaim the death that he suffered on the cross,
> we celebrate his resurrection, his bursting from the tomb,
> we rejoice that he reigns at your right hand on high
> and we long for his coming in glory.
> . . .
> As we recall the one, perfect sacrifice of our
>   redemption . . .   (Prayer F)

> Father, we plead with confidence
> his sacrifice made once for all upon the cross;
> we remember his dying and rising in glory,
> and we rejoice that he intercedes for us at your right hand.
>   (Prayer G)

Clearly this does not represent a new eucharistic theology, but the language is different and the emphasis has shifted.

No longer is it necessary to speak of 'our sacrifice of praise and thanksgiving', but it has now become proper to 'plead', indeed to 'plead with confidence', and 'memorial' has gone, to be replaced by 'remember', which, as the Church understands it, is a stronger word. It is easy to see a gentle shift.

The second area of difference is in relation to the picture painted of the life of heaven and our participation in the communion of saints. Prayer A simply unites our prayers 'with all who stand before you in earth and heaven'. Prayer B is stronger:

> . . . gather into one in your kingdom
> all who share this one bread and one cup,
> so that we, in the company of [N and] all the saints,
> may praise and glorify you for ever,

But Prayer C is silent on the subject. Taking the three together, reflecting as they do the *ASB* texts, this is an impoverished approach. Contrast that with the newer prayers.

> May we and all who share this food
> offer ourselves to live for you
> and be welcomed at your feast in heaven
>   where all creation worships you.   (Prayer D)

> Look with favour on your people,
> gather us in your loving arms
> and bring us with [N and] all the saints
> to feast at your table in heaven.   (Prayer E)

> Gather your people from the ends of the earth
> to feast with [N and] all your saints
> at the table in your kingdom,
> where the new creation is brought to perfection
> in Jesus Christ our Lord;   (Prayer F)

> Bring us at last with [N and] all the saints
> to the vision of that eternal splendour
> for which you have created us;
> through Jesus Christ, our Lord   (Prayer G)

Here are prayers that, while still giving weight to looking back to the last supper and the cross, celebrate the banquet of heaven and encourage the worshipper to look for and long for that perfect communion with God and with God's saints. The Eucharist emerges as a foretaste of heaven and that, especially for Anglicans whose liturgical formation has been with the Book of Common Prayer, is a truth they had not often encountered.

Another quite different feature of Order One Holy Communion has been the inclusion of shorter Eucharistic Prayers, Prayers D and H, the former part of the Liturgical Commission's original intention, the latter added at the revision stage in the General Synod. People requested such prayers for a variety of reasons. Brevity was the most common reason, suitability for occasions when children constitute a large part of the congregation was another, provision for communities where the literary language of the other prayers was unhelpful culturally was also sometimes sought, and sometimes the desire was voiced to have a prayer where the vocal participation of the congregation in the development of the prayer was greater.

The Commission's view had been that Prayer D met these needs. It is certainly briefer than the prayers already discussed. The Commission believed it would speak to children. The responsive form ('This is his/our story. This is our song.') enabled vocal congregational participation. Its language, though vivid, was simple and accessible:

> Almighty God, good Father to us all,
> your face is turned towards your world.
> In love you gave us Jesus your Son
> to rescue us from sin and death.
> Your Word goes out to call us home
>   to the city where angels sing your praise.
> We join with them in heaven's song.

The Synod thought otherwise. In relation to children it remained, after 2000, unhappy with the provision and commissioned further Eucharistic Prayers for children. In relation to participation and perhaps to length, it asked for a prayer where the words spoken by the congregation would match those of the president and where the congregational words, as much as the president's,

31

would move forward the logic of the prayer. What emerged was Prayer H, where every paragraph of presidential text led into two variable lines spoken by the whole congregation.

> When we turned away
> you did not reject us,
> but came to meet us in your Son.
> **You embraced us as your children**
> **and welcomed us to sit and eat with you.**

Opinions do, of course, differ on whether Prayer H is a valuable addition to the repertoire. Some welcome its brevity, others its vocal participation. But there is a good deal to regret. It abandons the classical shape of the prayer, which concludes with the Sanctus and without an 'Amen'. It misunderstands the nature of participation and plays into the hands of those who believe participation must be vocal, rather than prayerful. Because of its brevity, it is necessarily less rich in its theological themes. Crucially, because it requires so many different lines of response from the congregation, it requires attention to the text, rather than to the eucharistic action, throughout the prayer. Most seriously, it has become the normative prayer, indeed the only Eucharistic Prayer in use, in a number of churches. There are occasions when it might indeed be appropriate, but for it to be the only experience of a Eucharistic Prayer that some people are having is unfortunate indeed. Prayer D remains a far better option.

The question of responsive prayers remains an interesting one. The Eucharistic Prayer usually includes the Sanctus and Benedictus, the memorial acclamations and a doxology or great Amen, thus avoiding presidential monologue. But there has been pressure for more. Prayer A has an invariable response at the end of several paragraphs ('To you be glory and praise for ever'), Prayer D the story/song acclamation already mentioned; Prayer F has a series of acclamations, originating with the Eastern rite from which it is derived ('Amen. Lord, we believe', 'Amen. Come, Lord Jesus', 'Amen. Come Holy Spirit') and Prayer H has the responsive form discussed above. In Prayers A, D and F, these have been an enrichment and given the prayer a more dynamic style, but the responses need to be sung, as they are in some communities. They are best sung with a simple tune, unaccompanied, perhaps repeating the response after a deacon or cantor. Where they are spoken they can lack that dynamic quality and undermine the momentum of the prayer. Encouragement to sing is needed.

Indeed encouragement to sing is needed more widely. There are many churches where many hymns and songs are sung, even choir anthems performed during the distribution of communion, but where the key liturgical texts – Alleluia, Sanctus, Agnus Dei – are said, despite the provision of simple settings that do not require choir or organ. Where there is no singing the Eucharistic Prayer can seem long and, if not well led, wearisome. But the answer is often not to resort to as short a prayer as possible, but to recover the art of singing that lifts the prayer to another plane. There is a long way to go before this has been achieved.

A description of the use of the Eucharistic Prayers of *Common Worship* would be incomplete without mention of the 'extended Prefaces' for every season and holy day. Here are to be found some of the richest new material, drawing into the Eucharistic Prayer the story of the feast or the theological themes of the season being celebrated. Derived in many cases from contemporary Roman Catholic sources, they may replace the whole of the default Preface in Prayers A, B and E. Fairly widely and consistently used in some churches, they seem unknown in others, especially in churches with a full text of the Eucharistic Prayer set out in the local service book. They deserve more attention, none more so than an Extended Preface for the Sundays of Ordinary Time that is somewhat hidden away in the supplementary material. In the beauty of its language and the appeal of its theology, it illustrates what a treasury these Prefaces are.

> It is truly right and just, our duty and our salvation,
> always and everywhere to give you thanks,
> holy Father, almighty and eternal God.
> From sunrise to sunset this day is holy,
> for Christ has risen from the tomb

and scattered the darkness of death
with light that will not fade.
This day the risen Lord walks with your gathered people,
unfolds for us your word,
and makes himself known in the breaking of the bread.
And though the night will overtake this day
you summon us to live in endless light,
the never-ceasing sabbath of the Lord.
And so, with choirs of angels
and with all the heavenly host,
we proclaim your glory
and join their unending song of praise:
> Prefaces for the Sundays before Lent and after
> Trinity, Holy Communion, Supplementary Texts

Possibly the most significant change that the *Common Worship* eucharistic rite has brought about is a new unity across the traditions within the Church of England. Although there are Evangelical churches that sit light to any liturgical form and Anglo-Catholic churches that still insist that the Roman Catholic provision is better, both groups having little regard for canonical authority, the great majority of churches use the provisions of *Common Worship*, some slavishly, some creatively, but all in such a way that there is a family likeness to Anglican worship in England. Other than at the extremes, churchmanship does not seem to play a large part. Eucharistic prayers are not chosen for their theological subtleties, but for what seems pastorally appropriate. The Church of England seems happier and more united in its liturgy than it has been for many decades. *Common Worship*, despite all the variety and freedom it permits, has brought the Church back to common worship.

Note

1 Alternative Prayer for Penitence, Holy Communion, Order One, *Common Worship*. This and subsquent extracts in Chapter 1 are taken from the main volume, *Common Worship: Services and Prayers for the Church of England*, London, Church House Publishing, 2000.

2

Whatever happened to original sin?

Angela Tilby

———◆●◆———

Introduction

The slow, considered and consultative process which character-
izes liturgical revision in the Church of England often produces deeply impressive results. But there are occasions when
it leads to a change in theological perspective which would have
seemed dramatic had it happened all at once. Creeping up on
the Church in small instalments such a change can go unnoticed
with damaging results.

The most obvious example of this negative process is in
the baptism service, where the notion of baptism as effecting
a change from solidarity in sin to solidarity in the risen
Christ has been gradually but systematically eroded. The result
is a rite of thanksgiving and welcome with an underlying tone
of vaguely threatening moral demand which never really
expresses a theologically grounded view of what baptism is
about. These are large and possibly contentious claims – I will
try to justify them.

Baptism as part of Christian initiation

The publication of *Common Worship: Christian Initiation* in
2006 marked the culmination of one of the most difficult of
the *Common Worship* projects. There was one overriding object-
ive of the revision process, which was to re-envisage the whole
process of Christian initiation in the light of the central
importance of baptism. This followed the direction taken by
ecumenical discussions over many years and also followed new

approaches to Christian initiation in other parts of the Anglican Communion. The shape the revision took was largely influenced by *On the Way*, a paper 'on patterns of nurture in the faith, including the Catechumenate', requested by the General Synod in 1991 and published in 1995. This summarized years of debate on the relationship between baptism and confirmation, it reported on how the Catechumenate might be recovered, especially for adults and families, recognized the critical role of baptism in the Church's mission, and described the effect of diverse baptismal beliefs and practices within the Church of England. The work of revision was the first major task facing a new liturgical commission under David Stancliffe's chairmanship and is a reflection of new relationships that were being forged and new political realities being negotiated in the General Synod and elsewhere.

The project met a fair amount of criticism on the way, not least when draft services were brought to the General Synod for approval in 1995 and when revised versions were presented again in 1996. Some of the issues raised then are still around and have been the focus of requests for further revisions and a widening of options. In spite of problems there are few who would not acknowledge that the new initiation services have enriched the Church. The affirmation of baptism as the core of Christian identity has been enormously important, both ecumenically and within the diverse constituencies of the Church in England. The supporting rites 'on the way' for those preparing for baptism has made sense of a renewed catechumenate for adults and young people. The forms of penance seen as a recovery of baptism have helped the Church to recognize that baptism is the decisive step on a longer pilgrimage of faith which runs from cradle to grave. The predominance of Paschal imagery, 'dying and rising with Christ' has brought the Church closer to both its scriptural and its patristic sources. There has also been a widening of the metaphors employed for baptism which has enabled other important themes to be embraced, including those of liberation and deliverance. There is much more that can be said that is positive, not least the fact that the role of striking imagery is reinforced, ensuring that the rite of baptism is very much more than the liturgical texts.

Yet, for all the richness offered within this volume, I believe that the texts themselves do present a significant problem. I believe that they are open to the charge that they fail to give an adequate account of sin, especially that aspect of sin which is traditionally thought of as *inherited* as part of fallen human nature. The baptismal liturgy of the Church of England is now the expression of a significant doctrinal change away from what has up until now been shared with the Catholic and Reformed Churches.

The lack of clarity about what baptism effects

I should explain at this point that I came to this view by accident when looking for a pithy theological summary on the significance of baptism as the basis for a homily I had been asked to give at the baptism of the child of some friends in Cambridgeshire. I scanned the *Common Worship* introductory texts and commentaries, but though I found a range of explanations for what baptism is and what it means it was difficult to get any real clarity about what baptism is believed to effect in the lives of the candidates.

The language used in the Pastoral Introduction to the services of baptism in *Common Worship* is accessible enough but it is generally aspirational and gives little clarity of meaning.[1] Baptism is 'the beginning of a journey with God . . . the first step in response to God's love'. It is a 'joyful moment when we rejoice in what God has done for us in Christ'. It is a 'welcome' to a new Christian in which the wider community offers prayer and support. Sin is mentioned, but only in a subordinate clause: 'Our "drowning" in the water of baptism, where we believe we die to sin and are raised to new life, unites us to Christ's dying and rising . . '. All that is fine, and even poetic, but it does not quite break through the circle of church-speak. For why would we want to die and rise with Christ if there were not something inadequate about the way we are? What precisely does baptism do for the candidate other than introduce them to the inner circle of the already initiated?

I could not find in the texts, or in the commentaries, any equivalent to the elegant summary of the Book of Common Prayer Catechism (my emphasis):

> What is your Name?
> N. or M.
> Who gave you this Name?
> My Godfathers and Godmothers in my Baptism; wherein I was made *a member of Christ, the child of God, and an inheritor of the kingdom of heaven.*

The specificity of the BCP baptism service

The Prayer Book insists that baptism confers something not only real but specific, a particular status in relation to God: 'I was made *a member of Christ, the child of God and an inheritor of the kingdom of heaven*'. These phrases can all be traced back to scriptural sources, in particular to the Pauline letters, the Synoptic Gospels and most importantly to the Gospel of John. They closely echo themes found in patristic writers.

It is clear from this that the reformers of the English Church made theologically coherent choices about what baptism effected which they believed explained sufficiently why it was 'generally necessary for salvation'. From our perspective they did not say all that could be said, but they opted for coherence rather than comprehensiveness and the result is a text with a wonderfully tight-knit structure which expresses, above all, the fundamental seriousness of what is involved. The opening dialogue of the Catechism was the positive side of the redemptive drama that is played out in baptism; the rescuing of human nature from the corruption of inherited sin.

The theological position taken in The Ministration of Public Baptism of Infants is that baptismal regeneration is necessary for the removal of original sin. This is made clear in the opening exhortation, based on the work of Martin Bucer:

> Forasmuch as all men are conceived and born in sin, and that our Saviour Christ saith, none can enter into the kingdom of God, except he be regenerate and born anew of Water and of the Holy Ghost: I beseech you to call upon God the Father, through our Lord Jesus Christ, that of his bounteous mercy he will grant to this child that thing which by nature he cannot have; that he may be baptized with Water and the Holy Ghost, and received into Christ's holy Church, and be made a lively member of the same.

The Scripture passage which dominates the exhortation is the dialogue between Jesus and Nicodemus in John 3. This is introduced by an allusion to Psalm 51.5, 'in sin did my mother conceive me'. The combination of these texts provides the theological rationale for baptism. What is conferred on each child by the sacrament is *'that thing which by nature he cannot have'*. This is a very potent phrase. It insists that human nature is lacking in something vital for human fulfilment. The newborn child is brought into the church to have something done to him or her which is real and necessary. This can be stated negatively as the 'washing away of sin', or positively as the rebirth of water and the Spirit indicated by Jesus to Nicodemus. The rebirth supersedes natural birth, so that baptism does indeed confer the threefold status described in the Catechism as *a member of Christ, the child of God and an inheritor of the kingdom of heaven*.

All these terms are relational. Baptism brings the individual child beyond the common life of the natural order into the common life of the Church. 'Member of Christ' implies other members making up the one body of Christ (1 Corinthians 1.12), 'the child of God' identifies this and each child with Christ as Son of God, making explicit the Christian gift of 'sonship' or filiation in respect of each person. 'Inheritor of the kingdom of heaven' describes the baptized as an 'heir' of the promises originally given to Abraham and now open to all who have faith in Christ (Galatians 3.29—4.7).

Baptismal regeneration – the continuous tradition

The emphasis on sin and the need for rebirth is characteristic of most schools of Reformed theology and has roots in the ancient Church as it reflected on and interpreted Scripture. Baptism is a rebirth of water and Spirit, entry to the kingdom of God, light from darkness and the imparting of the knowledge of God, to which is added the main feature of John the Baptist's baptism as described in the Synoptic Gospels, a baptism 'of repentance for the forgiveness of sins'. The Fathers faithfully transmit these themes describing the necessity of baptism for 'regeneration, enlightenment, divine sonship, immortality, and remission of sins'. This list from Clement of Alexandria is fairly typical. Justin Martyr's famous description of baptism is as a 'bath of repentance and the knowledge of God effecting regeneration, illumination and remission of sins'. Belief in the forgiveness of sins is a clause in a number of early credal statements and the association of baptism with the forgiveness of sins was eventually incorporated into the Niceno-Constantinopolitan Creed.

The modern *Catechism of the Catholic Church* faithfully transmits these convictions in words which are surprisingly close to Bucer's exhortation: 'This sacrament is also called "the washing of regeneration and renewal by the Holy Spirit", for it signifies and actually brings about the birth of water and the Spirit without which no one "can enter the kingdom of God".'[2] The Catholic rite of 1976 has influenced the *Common Worship* baptism services in a number of ways, but with the significant difference that it does not hesitate to name the human problem which baptism addresses in terms of original sin. The *General Introduction to the Rites* says of those who are baptized, 'They are raised from their natural human condition to the dignity of adopted children.'[3] The prayer of exorcism normatively used at the baptism of children includes a specific petition that 'this child' or 'these children' should be 'set free from original sin'.

The embarrassment of sin

By contrast with the Fathers, the BCP and the modern Roman rite, the *Common Worship* baptism services seem embarrassed with the notion of sin, and where it is mentioned it is typically played down. The positive aspects of baptism do not balance the negative; they overwhelm them. I have already mentioned the relegation of 'sin' to a subordinate clause in the Pastoral Introduction. In the baptism service itself the Introduction of the liturgy (which may be replaced by suitable words from the president) retains a reference to the Nicodemus dialogue but it weakens it. Where the Gospel has Jesus saying 'no one can enter the kingdom of God without being born of water and the Spirit' (John 3.5), *Common Worship* has Jesus telling us that 'to enter the kingdom of heaven we must be born again of water and the Spirit'. There is no necessity or urgency here. The word 'sin' creeps in only in a present participle clause. 'Here we are clothed with Christ, *dying to sin* that we may live his risen life.' The implication of the way the sentence is phrased is that sin is to be renounced in order to live the risen life of Christ, not because it is dangerous or harmful in itself. There is no real sense that baptism might meet the thing that is *lacking* in human nature and put right something which nature cannot remedy.

The renunciations

As this Introduction provides the only mention of sin before The Decision the suddenly medieval tone of the first two renunciations, and the more banal but vaguely threatening tone of the third, come as something of a shock.

Do you reject the devil and all rebellion against God?
. . .
Do you renounce the deceit and corruption of evil?
. . .
Do you repent of the sins that separate us from God and neighbour?

41

The equivalent of this in the BCP is more grounded in the Bible and in the Christian spiritual tradition as a whole, asking at this point for a renunciation of the devil, the world, and the flesh. In patristic writings this pattern was frequently traced back to the three temptations of Christ in the wilderness; which culminate in Christ's refusal to submit to the devil, having subdued 'the world' by resisting the lure of world domination and the power of universal admiration, and 'the flesh' by resisting the temptation to turn stones to bread.

> Dost thou, in the name of this Child, renounce the devil and all his works, the vain pomp and glory of the world, with all covetous desires of the same, and the carnal desires of the flesh, so that thou wilt not follow, nor be led by them?

The significance of the echo of the experience of Christ is that the form of renunciation makes clear what *Common Worship* fails to express, that the solidarity with Christ in redemption is the reverse of the solidarity we share from birth with all humanity in human sin. The renunciations of baptism are not merely about personal sins, they are also about the transition from *natural* humanity, with its inherited tendency to sin, to fullness of humanity in Christ. *Common Worship* preserves the merest hint of this perspective in the second clause where 'the deceit and corruption of evil' is *renounced* rather than rejected. But the difference between this and the personal rejection of evil in the first clause is not altogether clear. The Prayer Book renunciations, on the other hand, are real renunciations, indicating the radical nature of the transition enacted in baptism with characteristic clarity and economy of expression.

The term The Decision, which replaces the notion of renunciation and has included, since the *ASB*, the positive aspects of turning to Christ, suggests by its very name that the grace of baptism is in some way triggered by the will of the candidate rather than by God. This is clearly not what is intended, but it could be the impression received.

Solidarity in sin and baptismal 'rescue'

In the BCP the scriptural witness to our human solidarity in sin is emphasized by the prayer that follows the first exhortation, a shortened version of a baptismal prayer of Martin Luther's which describes the place of baptism in the economy of salvation. The examples given are instructive. First, the prayer recalls Noah, saved with his family from perishing by water, and so from God's judgement on human sin. Second, the children of Israel are described as being 'led safely' through the Red Sea, prefiguring the salvation revealed in the baptism of Christ. The baptism of Christ is recollected as the place in which God 'didst sanctify water to the mystical washing away of sin'. The examples of Noah, the Red Sea and the baptism of Christ are cited in such a way as to underline the theme of rescue. Noah is saved from the flood, the Israelites are 'safely' led through the Red Sea. In both cases water is the element of destruction and danger. It is only with the baptism of Jesus that water becomes sanctified for its purpose of mystical washing and the giving of the Holy Spirit. Given this stress on rescue it is not surprising that baptism is seen primarily as the deliverance of the baptismal candidate from wrath.

The four solemn prayers are petitions directly related to the central theme of baptismal regeneration. The first asks that 'the old Adam in this child may be so buried, that the new man may be raised up in him'. The second requests the death of 'all carnal affections' and the life and growth of 'all things belonging to the Spirit'. The third asks for 'power and strength, to have victory, and to triumph against the devil, the world, and the flesh'. The fourth prayer is that all those present who have already been 'dedicated to thee by our office and ministry' may be 'endued with heavenly virtues, and everlastingly rewarded'.

Though *Common Worship* has much to say about our solidarity in the risen Christ, it has little to say about our pre-baptismal solidarity in the sin of the world. The solidarity with Christ is expressed in a number of ways. The prayer for the anointing of the Spirit after the actual baptism asks for daily renewal 'within the company of Christ's pilgrim people', the attractively worded address to the candidate at the Commission affirms that 'God has touched you with his love / and given you a place among his people', and goes on to say that 'together with all God's people / you must explore the way of Jesus / and grow in friendship with God, / in love for his people, / and in serving others. / With us you will listen to the word of God / and receive the gifts of God'.

This emphasis on the corporate nature of the life of the baptized is to be welcomed, but it is hard to see what it means theologically when it is not understood as the undoing and reverse of our solidarity in sin. Without this background it is all too easy to understand baptism more as a voluntary add-on to an already satisfactory life than as the God-given remedy for a fundamental flaw in human nature.

The erosion of original sin in the revisions of the baptism service

In fact, looking back over the revisions of the baptism service from the 1928 proposals to *Common Worship* we can trace a progressive deconstruction of the Prayer Book theology of baptism, grounded as it is in the conviction that sin is in some way inherited as part of the human condition. The 1928 Introduction removed the initial reference to men 'being conceived and born in sin' though in asking for baptismal regeneration it kept the important words, 'that which by nature he cannot have'. But subsequent and more recent revisions nagged away at this language, until we reached the point when it has almost entirely disappeared. The downplaying of sin is, of course, not only a feature of the baptismal services. It runs throughout the *Common Worship* provision and it is anticipated in the *ASB*. The result is that it is now perfectly possible to construct a Eucharist or Service of the Word in which sin and repentance are hardly mentioned at all. The loss of liturgical reference to sin began as a reaction against what came to be judged as the somewhat overstated concern of the BCP. The Catholic wing of the Church of England began a revolt against this with the 1928 Prayer Book revision and *Common Worship* is the final consequence. But while there is much to be commended in liturgy that affirms the life-giving and joyful aspects of faith, the downplaying of sin at baptism leads to particular problems.

The point at which this began to cause concern was with the baptism services in the *ASB*:

> Do you turn to Christ?
> **I turn to Christ.**
> Do you repent of your sins?
> **I repent of my sins.**
> Do you renounce evil?
> **I renounce evil.**   Baptism of Children

Evangelicals, always sensitive to the need to express our sinfulness before God, argued that the tone of the *ASB* baptismal renunciations lacked proper seriousness and weight. Various suggestions were offered as a corrective. The liturgical drafters offered phrases such as 'proud rebellion against God', and the 'glamour and corruption of evil', but these were excluded through the process of revision. Eventually a somewhat graver language than that in the *ASB* was employed, although the criticisms have not gone away, with some arguing that the *ASB* got it right, others wanting something sounding more contemporary and others preferring the draft version. I believe that the nagging dissatisfaction with The Decision is not with the language itself but with what it means, given that the context of renunciation of our fallen human nature is never adequately expressed. The adoption of a stronger tone for The Decision in *Common Worship* merely emphasizes the strangely jarring effect that any kind of renunciation of sin would have at this point.

Original sin – the wound of nature

It would be foolish to deny that the notion of original sin is hugely problematic in the form that it has been received by the

Western Church. The hardline Augustinian version of the doctrine is almost impossible to defend. For Augustine our solidarity with Adam in sin meant not only that human nature was corrupt but that each individual had a personal share in its guilt.

Augustine came to the view that baptism was necessary not only for the healing of the wound of nature but for the removal of the personal guilt that arose from inherited sin. There were Western writers before Augustine who had suggested this, basing their argument for inherited guilt on what we now recognize as an inaccurate understanding of Romans 5.12, 'Just as sin came into the world through one man, and death came through sin, and so death spread to all because [*eph' ho*] all have sinned . . .'. The most accurate representation of *eph' ho* is probably 'inasmuch as', rather than the NRSV's 'because'. But the old Latin version of this text mistranslated *eph' ho* as *in quo* 'in whom', and the 'whom' was taken to refer to Adam. Augustine pressed this faulty meaning to the limit and ended up with the horrible doctrine of limbo, the fate of unbaptized children after death, whose guilt made them incapable of being admitted to heaven. The mistranslation has now been universally acknowledged. The NRSV reads 'death spread to all *because* all have sinned' – a very different meaning. The Catholic Church recently distanced itself from this doctrine of limbo. But in the 1552 revision of the Book of Common Prayer the extreme Augustinian view was explicitly rejected by a rubric set out at the end of the baptism service: 'It is certain by God's Word, that children which are baptized before they commit actual sin, are undoubtedly saved.'

The Eastern Church could never have accepted Augustine's interpretation of original sin, but it does accept that Adam's sin has brought harm to humanity. As a result of this we are all prone to sin, easily dominated by the passions that arise from our earthly nature. Human mortality is the consequence of this. Death is not seen as it has been traditionally in the West, as a punishment for sin, but more as an act of divine mercy rescuing us from a corrupted immortality. Infants are baptized not because they have sinned, but because they, like all of us, are affected by sin. They are driven by appetite and desire, and prone to ignore or neglect the call to integration and union with God. As a consequence they are doomed to die. As I see it, that pretty well sums up the human condition.

A recognition of the wound that belongs to our natural humanity does not depend on a literal interpretation of the fall, or on the historic individuality of Adam. The point is that we experience being 'fallen', being diminished in our natural humanity and less than what we might be. The nag of conscience, idealism and aspiration remind us of what we could be and yet fail to be. I believe that it still makes sense to see baptism as the fundamental reorientation of our natural life away from the corruption, selfishness and greed which we inherit by nature, and towards Christ and his kingdom.

Much has been made of the recovery of a Paschal dimension to the *Common Worship* baptism services, but the Paschal mystery only makes sense against a realistic understanding of inherited sin. The 'fault' from which we are redeemed by such and so great a redeemer (to quote the *Exsultet* at the Paschal Vigil) might be a 'happy' one, but it is still a fault, a flaw.

The point here is that it has always been a part of Christian understanding, East and West, that sin is more than personal, it is part of universal human nature and so it really matters that we are able to give an intelligible account of it. Properly understood, original sin is a liberating doctrine. It frees us from the vanity and false innocence to which we are prone. It also frees us from an excessive moralism, an over-anxiety with our own effectiveness as redeemed believers.

But the coyness with which we treat inherited sin in contemporary liturgy suggests we have not understood this, or that we have simply stopped believing it. The baptismal renunciations of *Common Worship* and the surrounding prayers and exhortations are simply inadequate. Given that our base desires and appetites are constantly being provoked and manipulated by the dominant forces of contemporary society, and that the danger to our common life on earth by over-consumption and violence towards the created world threatens the well-being of every creature on the planet, this seems particularly unhelpful.

'The deceit' of evil has to stand for an awful lot. The Catholic rite is so much better at this point:

> Do you reject Satan?
> I do.
> And all his works?
> I do.
> And all his empty promises?
> I do.

The last phrase is particularly powerful, drawing together both scriptural memory of the 'empty promises' offered at Jesus' temptation, with the experienced 'empty promises' of a greedy society. It is simple, ancient, contemporary and absolutely relevant.

Denial of sin in the contemporary context

The Catholic rite also sets these simple but profound renunciations in a context in which inherited sin is acknowledged as the basic human problem. This is not the case with *Common Worship*, where the approach to sin mirrors too closely the superficial denial found in wider society. It was noted in *On the Way*, with reference to the report *Finding Faith Today* (1992), that 'there is very little sense of sin among a majority of those coming forward as adults for baptism/confirmation'.[4] This lack of a sense of sin was mentioned there without comment or interpretation.

Yet though it is true that a sense of sin is rarely articulated by people today, there are very obviously deep anxieties present in society which should be the subject of greater theological concern and reflection. These anxieties often arise from a sense of acute vulnerability and fragility which I find sometimes surfaces in conversations with parents bringing their children to baptism, especially with those who are not regular worshippers. A surprising number of such parents seek reassurance about the child's eternal destiny. Clergy and lay ministers may despair at their unsophisticated request to 'have the baby done'. But behind such sometimes faltering requests there is often a real awareness that the world is a dangerous and, indeed, a sinful place. Parents want to do all they can to ensure the physical and spiritual safety of their child. This puts ministers and other baptism visitors in a dilemma. Baptism is not a guarantee of good health or happiness and it cannot be reduced to a magic rite of protection. Out of the desire to counter what some will over-hastily judge as primitive or even pagan assumptions, ministers and lay visitors have perhaps over-stressed the ecclesial dimension of baptism, hoping thereby to bring parents as well as baby into committed membership of the Church while playing down any notion that baptism effects anything real. I have come to wonder whether the instincts of those who are less familiar with the ways of the Church are actually more theologically grounded than the apparently more optimistic account of human nature implied in *Common Worship*.

Without a robust understanding of inherited sin, baptism becomes a rather moralistic business, a demand disguised as a flattering affirmation that, after all, we belong to the nice and the good. This is most obvious in the optional Commission where the baptized are questioned about the sincerity of their intentions to live out their faith in the world. It is interesting that the Roman Catholic rite, while urging the parents of children to train their children in 'the faith', does not interpret the faith in the narrow terms of *Common Worship*, where it seems to be reduced to church membership and good behaviour.

This change from the understanding of baptism as necessary to salvation to the warm welcome ceremony to the church club has happened gradually. Yet the results are serious. We have ended up with a rite that casually edits out a central plank of Christian doctrine, a plank on which the whole logic of baptism itself depends. Anglicans tend to pride themselves on the rule *lex orandi, lex credendi*. But here it may have been applied rather too far and with a result which the bishops, as guardians of the faith of the Church, appear to have failed to notice. Without inherited sin what are the *Common Worship* baptism services really all about?

Notes

1 Extracts from *Common Worship* in this chapter are taken from *Common Worship: Christian Initiation*, London, Church House Publishing, 2005.

2 According to R. C. D. Jasper and Paul F. Bradshaw, *A Companion to the Alternative Service Book*, London, SPCK, 1986, p. 342.

3 International Commission on English in the Liturgy (trans.), *Rite of Baptism for Children* (1969), New York, Pueblo, 1976, p. 3.

4 *On the Way: Towards an Integrated Approach to Christian Initiation*, London, Church House Publishing, 1995, p. 21, citing John Finney, *Finding Faith Today*, Swindon, Bible Society, 1992.

3

The Common Worship
ordination services

ANDERS BERGQUIST

⸺•◆•⸺

The *Common Worship* ordination services came into use on 14
September 2005, following their final approval by the General
Synod in the previous July. This makes them one of the more
recent elements in the *Common Worship* project; they have been
in use for only five years, and any attempt to draw conclusions
from such a short history of use will have to be hesitant and
preliminary. There is not yet a body of experience to be examined
systematically, though there is occasional evidence from observed
practice in many cathedrals and churches that is suggestive.
This chapter will begin by revisiting some of the theologically
interesting questions that were raised in the sometimes lively
debates that took place during the process of synodical authorization, and ask where those questions stand in the light of
actual use. But neither has the Church of England stood still
in five years. Important developments in the way in which the
Church structures and articulates its ministry, which were being
developed at the same time as the ordination services were
under revision, are also coming into practical effect: one thinks,
for example, of the introduction of a category of Ordained
Pioneer Ministers, of the growth of Fresh Expressions regu-
lated by Bishop's Orders, and of the ways of thinking about
ministry that may be implicit in the clergy terms and conditions
of service that came into being in January 2011 under the
Ecclesiastical Offices (Terms of Service) Measure. How might
the ordination services be regarded in the light of these developments? Some reflection on these subjects may also be of interest

beyond the Church of England itself. Apart from its place within the Anglican Communion, it has many ecumenical partnerships, within England and beyond, and not least (through the Meissen Agreement) with Lutheran and Protestant churches in Germany, and (through the Porvoo Agreement), with Lutheran churches in Scandinavia and the Baltic states. Several of these are themselves embarking on a revision of their rites for commissioning or ordaining to formal ministries.[1]

Although this chapter will concentrate on the ordination services themselves, it is important to note at the outset that ordinations are not to be understood in isolation from other liturgical, or non-liturgical, actions that define and structure relationships within the Church. In ordination, a person is taken from within the body of the Church, and returned to that body in a new relationship, empowered to act in new ways so that the body may be built up. Deacons or priests do not cease to be members of the *laos* when they are ordained, but they are set apart within that *laos* to occupy particular roles, and to give practical expression to those roles in the performance of particular tasks. This set-apartness of the ordained within the *laos* is expressed in all sorts of ways, readily observable by a cultural anthropologist: in distinctive dress, for example, or in the occupying of particular parts of the church during a service into which others do not normally enter. It begins in the process of vocational discernment, especially in the Bishops' Advisory Panel (when the candidate goes away from home to undergo an intense and liturgically shaped experience which an anthropologist would recognize as a *rite de marge*, a liminal episode within a rite of passage).[2] It continues through the process of training, especially when training is residential (ordinands in college often feel that they have been abstracted from many of their earlier relationships and have, at least temporarily, 'lost' part of their earlier life; this sense of loss is a fundamentally healthy sign of engagement with the process leading towards ordination); and it deepens at the ordination retreat, which is most clearly a *rite de marge*. The ordination service can then be seen as the concluding rite of a long underlying process, and one in which the handing-back of the newly ordained to the Church may be a more important structural element than at first sight appears: though it may be cued by the bishop, the applause at the Welcome of the newly ordained usually feels warm and spontaneous, and has a deeper ritual logic than merely the expression of satisfaction or goodwill (in van Gennep's terms, it belongs to a *rite of aggregation*). The ordination is in turn followed by liturgical acts that continue what can be thought of as a single process. The new ministry is inaugurated in a particular place, for exercise in which it has been given: the new deacon is welcomed into a parish as its curate, the new priest presides for the first time at the Eucharist, the new bishop is welcomed into the diocese and inaugurates his new ministry in the cathedral church. Beyond these inaugurations, further licensings and institutions punctuate the lives of the ordained, until perhaps some special service of thanksgiving marks the laying-down of the work of consistent public ministry (the important complexities of the idea of 'retirement' in relation to ordained ministry need not be explored here). An ordination service is, then, properly understood as a single episode, though a pivotal one, within a much longer sequence that has a liturgical structure as a whole.

Baptism and vocation

Each of the *Common Worship* ordination services begins with a reminder that all Christ's people have a calling:

> God calls his people to follow Christ, and forms us into a royal priesthood, a holy nation . . . In baptism, the whole Church is summoned to witness to God's love and to work for the coming of his kingdom.[3]

The bishop (or archbishop) then continues:

> To serve this royal priesthood, God has given a variety of ministries. Deacons [or priests, or bishops] are ordained so that . . .

It is helpful to be reminded what is, and what is not, being said in this theologically foundational statement, deliberately placed at the opening of the service. Ordained ministry is dependent on a prior reality, out of which it grows and which it exists to serve: the royal priesthood of Christ's people. Every Christian is baptized into this royal priesthood, and in that sense baptism is also a call to ministry for every Christian, but the word 'ministry', in 'the ministry of all baptized Christians', is not identical with the word 'ministry', in 'the ministry of the ordained', and they are not to be played off against one another as alternatives. The ministry of the ordained exists to articulate, to structure and to serve the ministry of all the baptized. The idea of the priesthood of all Christ's people is theologically prior to, but is not inimical to, the idea of a priesthood to which particular people may be ordained within the life of the Church. The *Common Worship* ordination services may therefore be said to begin with a statement of 'baptismal ecclesiology' or 'every-member ministry', but not in a sense that undercuts the reality and distinctiveness of ordained ministry within the body of the Church. How far has this understanding of baptismal calling as the context of a call to ordained ministry been expressed liturgically in the performance of *Common Worship* ordination services? Three practices have been observed:

1 The bishop may give the greeting and introduction from the font, where the prayers of penitence may also appropriately be said, before moving in procession through the nave for the presentation of the candidates. The practicality of this depends obviously on the location of the font within the building: cathedrals which have been reordered with the font placed centrally near the west door will lend themselves more easily to this articulation of the rite.

2 The candidates, rather than entering the church in procession 'from outside' at the beginning of the service, may at first be seated within the congregation. They are then called out from the midst of the people, to be presented to the bishop for

ordination. Their physical movement from the body of the congregation to stand before both the bishop and the people gives symbolic expression to the idea that the ministry of the whole people is the matrix out of which their ordained ministry emerges.

3 The candidates may be brought before the bishop by members of the *laos* (lay or ordained) who have had a particular role in encouraging them along the vocational journey which has brought them to this point. This emphasizes the way in which the journey is always an accompanied one, made within the body from which the individual now comes to be ordained. In the Church of England, ordination is both universal and particular. It is not circumscribed by a particular place or community, but it is always *to* a particular context: there is never 'absolute ordination', in the sense of an ordination made without explicit reference to the particular place or community for the service of which the universal gift of order is given. But ordination is also always *from* a particular context. It was decided by the General Synod, in the course of the debates on the *Common Worship* ordination services, that candidates should continue to be presented formally to the bishop by the archdeacon, or a representative of the archdeacon (cf. Canon C.18.1). Many dioceses have found ways of preceding this formal presentation by a movement that expresses wordlessly the emergence of a vocation from within the body of the Church in an accompanied way.

Vocation to ordained ministry is, then, a calling from, as well as a calling towards. It has a second double aspect: it is discerned by the Church, and it is felt by the individual. The relationship between an individual's interior sense of being called, and the Church's extrinsic discernment of a call, were much discussed during the revision of the *Common Worship* ordination services. The solution arrived at was to postpone the bishop's question to the ordinand:

Do you believe that God is calling you to this ministry?

until after he has first asked 'those whose duty it is to know [them] and examine them' whether they believe them to be duly called to this ministry.

For the first time in the Church of England's practice, and in contrast to both the BCP and *ASB* ordinals,[4] a declaration by representatives of the Church that a vocation has been discerned is explicitly made *before* the ordinand is (in effect) asked whether this extrinsic discernment finds a corresponding movement in his or her own heart. The *Common Worship* ordination services are, further, careful never to use words that assume that the ordination will in fact take place until the congregation has heard the bishop describe the ministry to which the ordinands are to be ordained, has heard them make their promises and undertakings in relation to that ministry, and has given its consent. Before every ordination, in other words, a vocation must have been discerned by competent authority, this discernment must find an interior response in each individual ordinand, and the whole people who are gathered around the bishop to celebrate the ordination must give their consent. One might suggest that the welcome given by the people through their applause after the ordination is another expression of that consent, and so has a theological significance, as have the rites by which the new ministry is later inaugurated in practice.

Ordination through prayer with the laying on of hands

In the *Common Worship* ordination services, the central action of the rite is presented as a continuous sequence of prayer, which begins with a call to silent prayer, continues (for the ordination of priests and bishops) with the singing of *Veni Creator*, progresses through the Litany, and culminates in the Ordination Prayer, during which hands are laid on the head of each person to be ordained. Three observations may be made about currently observed practice in relation to this part of the rite.

The laying on of hands

There are many references in the New Testament to the laying on of hands with prayer, sometimes in contexts to do with commissioning for mission and ministry, sometimes for other purposes such as healing. The exact role of the laying on of hands (usually of the right hand) in appointment to minister-ial office in early Christian centuries is not well understood, partly because the evidence is scattered, and partly because there seems to have been a variety of understanding and practice: in this, as in other areas of liturgy, the notion of a consistent patristic practice that can act as a precedent for contemporary use is an illusion.[5] But whatever its earlier history, a prayer of invocation of the Holy Spirit, accompanied by the laying on of hands, became the central and distinctive feature of ordination rites in Churches of both East and West. In the Church of England, as in the Roman Catholic and Orthodox Churches, the combination of the invocation of the Holy Spirit with the laying on of hands has, in commissioning to ministries, been reserved to ordinations, though the gesture of the laying on of hands has, of course, continued to be used in other settings, such as confirmations, blessings and healing services. This distinctive feature of ordinations is now some-times also observed at services of commissioning to other, non-ordained, ministries. The process of extension is easily accounted for by a proper desire that such ministries should not be perceived as somehow 'second best'. If a formally commissioned lay ministry is one of real responsibility and significance within the life of the Church of England, then it might seem that people should be commissioned to that ministry with all the resources of prayer that the Church is capable of. But there may be an unintended consequence, which is worth considering. If lay ministers are commissioned to their ministries in a way that exactly matches the way in which ordained ministers are ordained to their ministries, with the invocation of the Holy Spirit in similar terms, and the identical gesture of the laying on of hands, would it not appear that their ministries are ordained ministries? And what would be the consequences for the Church of England's continuing and strongly expressed commitment to the threefold order of bishop, priest and deacon? A similar problem surfaces in other areas of practice, in a way not sufficiently recognized. For many lay readers, the notion of the lay character of their ministry is central to their ministerial self-understanding, but if in the performance of their duties they wear distinctive dress that is more like the dress of the clergy than it is like everyday wear, and if they occupy particular spaces in the church that are commonly occupied by clergy, and if they undertake specialized liturgical roles similar to those undertaken by clergy, then to an outside observer they will seem to be clergy. Those who are highly acculturated to the system may know that there is an important difference between a blue preaching scarf and a black one, but to those innocent of these codes, the lay minister seems to be set apart in the same way as the ordained one. The practice, technically irregular but easily understandable, of the laying on of hands at the commissioning of some lay ministers may be seen as a symptom of the clericalization of lay ministries – and ought logically to be resisted by those who cherish the distinctively lay character of such ministries.

The role of the college of presbyters

The *Common Worship* ordination services continue the Church of England's existing practice, that the bishop alone lays his hands on those ordained deacon, but that priests assist in laying hands on those ordained priest. The Canons insist on this: interestingly, not as a thing that may be done, but as one that must be done:

> The priests taking part in an ordination *shall together with the bishop* lay their hands upon the head of every person who receives the order of priesthood. (Canon C.3.4; my emphasis)

This implies that the laying on of hands by the participating priests is more than simply a confirmatory practice, which does no more than underscore what the bishop has sufficiently done by himself. It is intrinsic to the ordination. The bishop presides over the gathering of the whole people, and he presides over the college of presbyters within the diocese. In adding new priests to that college under the bishop's presidency, the college itself takes an active part. This is why the practical guide in the study edition of the *Common Worship* ordination services is at pains to point out that the priests who assist in the laying on of hands should not simply represent the friends and supporters of this or that individual ordinand, but should be a visible sign of the body of priests within the diocese, and that the assisting priests should lay their hands on the head of every ordinand, and not only on those with whom they have a personal connection. Whether 'together with the bishop' has to mean 'simultaneously with the bishop' is more doubtful, though the usual practice in the Church of England is still for the ordinand to be lost from view under a crowd of outstretched arms. The usual Roman Catholic practice, in which the assisting priests lay on hands individually, in succession, during a period of silence, can create a powerful sense of Spirit-filled stillness. The fact that deacons were in early Christian centuries understood as holders of an office closely linked to the bishop, rather than as members of a collegiate body, explains why the custom arose that the bishop alone laid his hands on those ordained deacon.

An unbroken sequence of prayer

The Prayer Book moves away from the unbroken sequence of prayer, by inserting a formula addressed to the ordinand:

> Take thou authority . . .
>
> The Form and Manner of Ordering of Priests

As this is an injunction and not a prayer, delivered solemnly to the ordinand by the bishop, it was natural for the bishop to speak the words while seated in his chair, and – once the wearing of mitres was usual again at ordinations, which was not until well into the twentieth century – to wear his mitre as he spoke them. This image of the bishop, seated and mitred as he confers orders, is itself a revival of a medieval image, and has remained surprisingly persistent, although it is clearly at odds with the Ordination Prayer as presented in *Common Worship*. As a prayer, it would normally be prayed without mitre. And while the different phases of the unbroken sequence of prayer might be articulated by changing from one position of prayer to another – kneeling for the opening silence, the *Veni Creator* and the Litany, and then standing for the Ordination Prayer – it is strange for any part of the prayer to be prayed seated. It is probable that this disjunction between the logic of the prayer and some current practice will disappear over time; a persistent liturgical habit will eventually disappear when it has no soil, in the structure of the rite, in which to flourish.

The Giving of the Bible

The Giving of the Bible, or more accurately the giving of a New Testament to deacons and of a Bible to priests and bishops, has been a load-bearing component of ordination services in the Church of England since the Reformation, and no feature of the draft *Common Worship* ordination services caused as much controversy as the suggestion that the Bible might be given as part of a *missio* at the conclusion of the service, rather than in its traditional place immediately after the Ordination Prayer. The final text provides for the Bible to be given in either place, and the merits and demerits of either position can still be debated. To place the Giving of the Bible as close as possible to the Ordination Prayer is to give powerful symbolic emphasis to the authority that is being given, by a church that sees itself as under Scripture, to preach the word of God and to celebrate the sacraments of the New Covenant. But this symbolism is partly lost when the newly given Bible immediately has to be given to someone else to look after, or put away on a chair, because the newly ordained owner of it needs both hands to exchange the Peace, or has to get on with preparing the holy table. To make the Giving of the Bible part of a sending out at the end of the service is to emphasize that it is the foundation and tool of mission – it is to go with the newly ordained as they are sent out to proclaim the kingdom. Both practices are now found. What is seldom found is the taking up of the possibility, allowed for in *Common Worship*, that when the Giving of the Bible takes place immediately after the Ordination Prayer, a single large Bible may be used. This would symbolically be the Church's Bible, rather than the Bible of the individual minister, and would presumably be the Bible from which the newly ordained would read publicly if there were readings still to be read. In the background is the older custom of giving to the newly ordained deacon a Book of the Gospels, from which he would read at a later stage of the liturgy. In the Prayer Book, the New Testament replaced the Book of the Gospels, but the tradition that it was for immediate use persisted: one of the new deacons (in the nineteenth and early twentieth centuries, usually the one who had scored the highest marks in the written ordination examination) would read the Gospel at the Communion Service that immediately followed the ordination. If a single large Bible is given, then individual Bibles have to be given, without words, at the end of the service. It may be that the consequent duplication of Bible-giving has been thought undesirable or confusing. But it may also be that the idea of the individual copy, to be cherished and used throughout a person's ministry, has become more deeply rooted in the Church of England than the idea of the giving of the shared book for use in the community. The primacy of this individual scriptural piety (and the phrase is intended entirely without negative connotation) is suggested by an interesting way in which the provision of *Common Worship* is sometimes disregarded. The BCP Ordinal, and the *ASB* after it, gave the New Testament to deacons, and the whole Bible to priests. This may or may not be related to the way in which the BCP Ordinal presents the diaconate as a kind of testing-ground, in which deacons may prove themselves fit for the priesthood.[6] At all events, it can appear strange: are not deacons meant to teach from the Old Testament also? So *Common Worship* directs that deacons too should be given a complete Bible. The Church of England has, however, had a custom, rooted in a loving concentration on the study of the Greek text of the New Testament in the tradition of Westcott, Hort, Lightfoot and others, of giving the New Testament in Greek. This custom is proving remarkably – some would say, encouragingly – resilient. Many ordaining bishops still have the Greek NT that they were themselves given when they were ordained deacon, and continue to give them to their own ordinands.

Epilogue

Like the *ASB* Ordinal, the *Common Worship* ordination services are alternative to those in the BCP, although in practice the BCP is little used. It presents some particular challenges in practice; the full sequence (which it assumes) of Morning Prayer and Litany, followed by the Ordination, followed by a service of Holy Communion, is thought to be long by a twenty-first-century congregation. But it would be a diminution of the Church of England's life if it were to fall altogether into disuse, and it is much to be hoped that bishops might occasionally use it for an ordination, or choose it for their own consecration. One of its striking features, worth retaining as a living part of the Church of England's life, is its honesty about the human frailty of candidates. Before ordaining a priest, the bishop asks the congregation whether any of them wishes to allege 'any impediment or notable crime' – lesser crimes are presumably to be taken in the Church's stride. As the archbishop hands the Bible to the newly consecrated bishop, he enjoins him to 'be to the flock of Christ a shepherd, not a wolf; feed them, devour them not' (from The Form of Ordaining or Consecrating of an Archbishop or Bishop). The prescribed readings (for example, 1 Timothy 3.8–13 for the ordination of deacons, 1 Timothy 3.1–7 for the consecration of a bishop) have a straightforward practicality about them: no prophetic Call Narratives here, or profound Pauline reflection on the nature of the Church, but reminders to be hospitable, and to beware of the bottle and too much concern with money. This is a healthy counterweight to what one might call an idealizing tendency in modern ordination services.

At the same time, the *Common Worship* ordination services can be seen as having a special importance, in the context of the increasing prevalence of a discourse about ordained ministry which sees it as a category of employment, to be organized, appraised and resourced on the analogy of secular employment. This process is driven by many factors, some of them extrinsic, such as the requirements of secular law, and some of them broadly cultural, such as the assumption that best practice in commercial life is the model for best practice in every kind of organization. Here is not a place to enter into a discussion of an important wider issue in the Church of England's life. What is not in doubt is that good employment practice, as it is understood in secular workplaces and tribunals, is increasingly shaping the working conditions under which the ordained exercise ministries in practice; the Clergy Conditions and Terms of Service which came into force at the beginning of 2011 are a particular milestone in a process which extends much further back, at least as far as the creation of a unified stipend system, and which will extend further into the future. The ordination services themselves – their text, and their practice as actual liturgical events – provide an essential framework within which discussion about conditions and terms of service has to be located, because they recall us constantly away from the particularity of doing a particular job, to wider themes of vocation, and role, and the shaping of human lives by God. This is especially true when the ordination services are themselves seen to be one element within a liturgical process that extends from vocation to retirement and beyond.

At the same time, the ordination services provide an important focus of unity at a time when the articulation of ordained ministry within the Church of England is becoming more diverse. Some are ordained to a title with a stipend, some to one without; some are ordained with the expectation that they will move to positions of responsibility and incumbency, and others with the expectation that theirs will be a supporting pastoral ministry; some are ordained to a ministry in a parish, or in a fresh expression of church, or in a secular workplace. But the order to which they are ordained is not differentiated, and the rite by which they are ordained is the same for them all. To paraphrase Gertrude Stein, a priest is a priest is a priest; and the fact that they are, for all the variety of the particular ways in which they will minister, ordained with the same rite, is a powerful reminder of that equality.

Notes

1 Cf. Irene Mildenberger and Wolfgang Ratzmann (eds), *Ordinations-verständnis und Ordinationsliturgie: ökumenische Einblick*, Leipzig, Evangelische Verlagsanstalt, 2007; Hans Raun Iversen (ed.), *Rites of Ordination and Commitment in the Churches of the Nordic Countries: Theology and Terminology*, Copenhagen, Museum Tusculanum Press, 2006.

2 Arnold van Gennep's classic *Les Rites de Passage*, which first appeared in 1909 and has been translated into English several times, should be read by anyone who has to organize an ordination service.

3 Extracts from *Common Worship* in this chapter are taken from *Common Worship: Ordination Services, Study Edition*, London, Church House Publishing, 2007.

4 The first Anglican 'Form and Manner of Making, Ordaining and Consecrating of Bishops, Priests, and Deacons' appeared in 1550 and 1552, separately from the Book of Common Prayer, but later came to be bound in with the Prayer Book. The term 'BCP Ordinal' is used here as convenient shorthand for the ordination services to be found in any copy of the 1662 Book of Common Prayer.

5 Cf. for ordination services, Paul Bradshaw, *Ancient Ordination Rites of East and West*, New York, Pueblo, 1990, and more generally, Paul Bradshaw, *Reconstructing Early Christian Worship*, London, SPCK, 2009. Although there is variation in early Christian practice in commissioning readers, one can see traces of a shared principle that the laying on of hands is a sign of a person's being ordained to the clergy. In the *Apostolic Constitutions* (late fourth century Syria?), the reader is ordained by the invocation of the Holy Spirit and the laying on of hands, with an explicit expectation that he will go on to 'be declared worthy of a higher degree' (8.22): becoming a reader is a step onto a clerical ladder. In *Apostolic Tradition* (11),

by contrast, which at this point may reflect an alternative Eastern tradition rather than a Western one, 'the reader is appointed by the bishop's giving him a book; for hands are not imposed'. Cf. Paul Bradshaw, Maxwell Johnson and Edward Phillips, *The Apostolic Tradition: A Commentary*, Minneapolis, Fortress Press, 2002, pp. 75–6; Harry Gamble, *Books and Readers in the Early Church*, New Haven and London, Yale University Press, pp. 221–2.

6 Cf. the bishop's prayer after communion, that the new deacons 'may so well behave themselves in this inferior office, that they may be found worthy to be called unto the higher ministries in thy Church . . .' (from The Form and Manner of Making of Deacons).

4

A Service of the Word

JEREMY FLETCHER

———•◦•———

The Liturgical Commission of the 1980s was unusually busy. In his Presidential Address to the General Synod in July 1980 the Archbishop of Canterbury, Robert Runcie, had said that 'We stand at a point where the heroic era of constitutional and liturgical change is over.'[1] Ten years later the Commission had produced *Lent, Holy Week, Easter* (1984), *Patterns for Worship* (1989), and *The Promise of His Glory* (1989).

Each of these publications broke ground which laid essential foundations for the next two decades of liturgical change. *Lent, Holy Week, Easter* introduced a wealth of seasonal material which, though in the guise of fully worked-out services, marked the beginning of the 'directory' model, providing resources which could be used flexibly rather than in a uniform way. *The Promise of His Glory* took this approach much further, with a greater range of material for the seasons from Advent to Candlemas, and proposing changes to the liturgical year, including a putative 'Kingdom' season. It may well be thought that *Patterns for Worship* will be seen to be the most radical of all the offerings of that 1980s Liturgical Commission. Not only did it contain material which would influence the provision of the Eucharist in *Common Worship*, it proposed the flexible use of the lectionary ('open' and 'closed' seasons, enabling churches legally to depart from required readings on Sundays), and, most radically of all, it offered a service which contained no texts whatsoever.

On first sight A Service of the Word, which was finally authorized as an alternative to Morning and Evening Prayer in

1993, does not look like anything to frighten the liturgical horses. The authorized material is a little over four pages, containing simply a series of headings with explanatory notes. In this unassuming form, however, can be discovered many of the principles which underlie *Common Worship* and the current liturgical practice of the Church of England. Though many of these were prefigured in the *Alternative Service Book*, A Service of the Word both made them clear and also encouraged an enormous range of liturgical development. Chief among them was an entirely new approach to the planning of an act of worship. A Service of the Word provided nothing but a structure (and a flexible one at that). The leader of worship was now required to shape and flesh out the service to be led.

Planning worship: from reaction to action

Twenty years after *Patterns for Worship* was first published it is hard to remember what it was like to begin to plan an act of worship in the early 1980s. The *ASB* looked like the BCP. It was full of worked-out services, had readings and prayers for the whole of the church year, and was commended to me only recently as the kind of 'one stop shop' which could, like the BCP, be used for all a worshipper's public and private devotional needs. To plan worship in the era of the *ASB* was to give thanks for those who had put together such a wealth of material, take the services provided, and (perhaps) make use of the alternative texts at certain points. Holy Communion and Morning and Evening Prayer were set out clearly, allowing for a measure of seasonal variation, with all the texts neatly in place. Choice was limited to language (contemporary or traditional for the Eucharist; traditional or contemporary settings of the canticles in Morning and Evening Prayer), or alternative texts at particular points (such as the Confession, or the Prayer of Humble Access). Essentially the planner of worship would start with the text as it was, insert hymns, and perhaps take out one set text and replace it with another. It was entirely possible to open *ASB* Rite A at page 119, and continue without too much trouble to page 145. Most things were done for you.

But even here the revolution was brewing. There was, for example, that interesting rubric 'in these or other suitable words'. Careful investigation revealed that, though there were approved alternative texts in some cases, 'suitable' could also include words made up locally for the occasion. This did prompt the question as to what was 'suitable' and who might be the arbiter should there be a dispute, but in allowing in this way for the one-off and the local the *ASB* opened a door which would be pushed wide open by A Service of the Word. And though it may have *looked* like the BCP, there was actually a vast range of choice. In the Eucharist the initial choice was between Rites A and B, and then, in Rite A for example, a choice of prayers of Confession, Humble Access, Post Communion and, most radically for the time, up to six Eucharistic Prayers. Though a richer observance of the Church's year had been a developing feature throughout the twentieth century for the Church of England, it was the *ASB* which collected together many of the texts and observances which had been in use, and introduced them to the Church as a whole. It even proposed a new beginning to the year, starting at the Ninth Sunday before Christmas, and opening up the possibility of new shapes within the classic calendar. Not all our structures were written in stone, it seemed.[2]

Most importantly for this discussion, the *ASB* made a great feature of the *structure* of the service. Again this was seen most clearly in the Eucharist. The main headings drew attention to the basic shape of the service:

- Preparation
- Ministry of the Word
- Ministry of the Sacrament
- Dismissal

Within that overall structure was a commitment to reveal the 'shape' of the Eucharist itself:

- Taking
- Thanksgiving
- Breaking
- Distributing

This may not have been noticed by every worshipper, but in starting with an agreed structure and then fleshing out that structure with suitable texts the *ASB* began the process which would lead to the structure being the key feature of each service in *Common Worship*. The structure page in *Common Worship* defines the service, and the texts which follow are but one example of how that structure might be worked out.

In the early 1980s our eagle-eyed worship planner thus had some official publications which were giving a nudge to a change of the starting-point in the planning of worship. Structures, alternatives and local options were all now a part of the provision. A Report to General Synod called *The Worship of the Church* in 1986 noted that these freedoms were hinted at by *ASB* but not being utilized. New writing could 'give encouragement to the "loosening up" which the *ASB* 1980 clearly had in mind but of which real advantage is yet to be taken'.[3] What A Service of the Word was then to make absolutely clear was that the beginning of the process of planning an act of worship should not be a full text provided beforehand by someone else, but a shape and structure, refined for the local context, fleshed out by elements only some of which had to be authorized by the 'centre'. It is a measure of the success of this project that this now seems the obvious place to start. A Service of the Word made it so, but did not do so simply because it seemed like a good idea to some liturgists or the House of Bishops. A number of factors were involved.

Antecedents of A Service of the Word

Patterns for Worship offered three reasons for its publication. The first was that the *ASB* should not be seen as the end of a process first begun in 1965 (and indeed looking back 400 years), but should also be seen as looking forward 'to a new era of flexibility in the Church of England [*sic*] worship'.[4] There were then two pressing needs in the current life of the Church. The *Faith in the City* report had made it plain that offering a 1300-page book to worshippers in an urban context was an unhelpful and counterproductive thing to do. What was needed for these places was worship which was still Anglican but much more attuned to different linguistic registers, and able to be light on its feet, relating clearly to a very local context. The report called for 'short, functional' booklets or cards, and for writing which was 'concrete and tangible' rather than 'abstract and theoretical'. Crucially *Patterns for Worship* says that defined local needs are not best met by 'a group of experts at the centre laying down all the words of the liturgy', but by the creation of a framework to enable the creation of 'genuinely local liturgy'.[5] Though the needs of Urban Priority Area parishes were uppermost in the Liturgical Commission's mind, the principle of enabling a structure for liturgy to be done appropriately for the local context is one which should be applied to every aspect of the Church of England's worship and mission.

The other pressing need to be met was the recognition that the 'Family Service' movement had come of age. Non-eucharistic services with a simple structure, concrete language and the aim of including people of all ages and cultures have a long history in the Church of England. Permission was given in 1872 to allow a 'Third Service' which did not have to be Matins, Evensong or Communion (but could only use BCP texts and words from the Bible). This was an attempt to give some flexibility in worship to a Church stunned by the recognition from the 1851 census that the majority of people did not attend worship regularly. In 1892 permission was broadened to allow other material 'substantially in agreement with Scripture and the *Prayer Book*'.[6] Legally, at least, this remained the official position of the Church of England until the authorization of A Service of the Word in 1993.[7]

Under these reasonably restricting provisions a new movement flourished. Sunday Schools began to hold services in parallel to the authorized ones, and in other places the 'main' service was designed to incorporate all ages in a format based on, but not the same as, Morning Prayer. By 1968 the Church Pastoral Aid Society had produced its *Family Service* (derived from a shortened form of Morning Prayer) and in 1986 their *Church Family Worship* offered some sample services and hundreds of prayers and songs in a 'directory' format. What concerned the Liturgical Commission were the reflections of people like Nigel McCulloch, then Bishop of Taunton, who wrote in 1986 that the best attended services in many churches were ones which had little liturgical or theological underpinning, and the report by the Diocese of Chelmsford called *For Families* (also 1986), which pointed out many dangers as well as obvious strengths.[8]

The Liturgical Commission wanted to harness the obvious energy of the 'Family Service' movement, and to enable it to be not parallel to, but obviously at the centre of, the Church's worship. Though earlier writing had talked about family services being a 'bridge' over which non-attenders might walk into the full worshipping life of the Church,[9] *Patterns for Worship* contented itself with a reference to the bridge being something where the Church might express its worship in a proper reflection of 'local culture'.[10] Indeed, a well-framed intergenerational service might well introduce regular worshippers to other aspects of worship, enable people to develop gifts of planning and leading worship, enable creative means of communicating the word and provide a less conservative context for new music to be introduced. An engagement with the Family Service movement was not about a reining-in of miscreants, but an enlivening of the existing worship of the Church as well.

The principles of A Service of the Word

The *ASB* had opened up the possibility of more flexibility than there had been before, and the unlocking of the gate was an opportunity waiting to be grasped. Many churches were finding that their best attended service was one which had little if any relationship to the official liturgical provision of the Church of England, and *Faith in the City* called for better and more relevant worship resources for the Church's mission in urban areas. In addition, the report *Children in the Way* (1988) asked for much the same thing, adding to the pressure of the Family Service movement. The Commission's response was *Patterns for Worship*, and, at its heart, A Service of the Word. The piece of liturgical genius, the proposition which completely changed the nature of liturgical development in the Church of England, is that the starting-point of all future writing of liturgy would be the structure, style and principles of worship, not the text *per se*. Where before it had been possible to agree full texts which conformed to the authorization processes of the Church of England, now what was important was to define the principles on which texts would be based, and then allow the local, not the national, church to put them into practice. In crude terms the Holy Trinity of the Liturgical Commission, the House of Bishops and the General Synod would become the servant, not the master, of the worship of the local church Sunday by Sunday.

Patterns for Worship therefore began by proposing the underlying principles, or 'marks', of Anglican worship, which any act of worship in the name of the Church of England should display. In a list which became much used and oft repeated these were:

- a recognizable structure for worship
- an emphasis on reading the word and using psalms
- liturgical words repeated by the congregation, some of which, like the creed, would be known by heart
- using a Collect, the Lord's Prayer, and some responsive forms in prayer
- a recognition of the centrality of the Eucharist
- a concern for form, dignity and economy of words.[11]

Using these principles as a basis, the Commission then provided what they regarded as the essential elements of a structure for any 'word' service, be it a version of Morning or Evening Prayer, a 'Family' Service or the first part of Holy Communion. Again, a principle underpinned the structure: that there should be a *balance* of elements. In the Introduction to *Patterns* the four elements are listed as 'word, praise, prayer and teaching'.[12] In the 'Instructions for The Service of the Word' the four elements become 'word, praise, prayer and action'.[13] The Commission recognized that 'action' was more difficult to define than the other three, and that it would often be 'done at the same time as one of them'.[14] Initial texts mention the lighting of candles, movement of the congregation from one place to another, or the reading of the Bible being done in dramatic form; the final text approved in 1999 simply spoke of a balance between 'congregational activity and . . . passivity'.[15] The need for balance is repeated throughout *Patterns*, especially in the Commentary material, presumably in response to the observed weaknesses of family services and other liturgies of the time.

A Service of the Word then specifies the required elements of any service. The six sections in *Patterns* (Introduction; Penitence; Praise; The Word; Prayers; Ending) eventually became four: Preparation; Liturgy of the Word; Prayers; Conclusion. Its final form is printed below, with required elements in bold. Permission is given for items to be placed in any order, with some items happening more than once if appropriate.

Preparation

The minister welcomes the people with the **Greeting. Authorized Prayers of Penitence** may be used here or in the **Prayers.** The Venite, Kyries, Gloria, a hymn, song, or a set of responses may be used. The **Collect** is said either here or in the **Prayers.**

The Liturgy of the Word

This includes **readings (or a reading) from Holy Scripture;** a **psalm,** or, if occasion demands, a scriptural song; a **sermon;** an **authorized Creed,** or, if occasion demands, an **authorized Affirmation of Faith.**

Prayers

These include **intercessions and thanksgivings** and **the Lord's Prayer.**

Conclusion

The service concludes with a **blessing, dismissal** or other **liturgical ending.**

The revolution here is not in the use of any individual element, but in the fact that the structure was intentionally flexible, and that trust was placed in the end-user to act with common sense and theological and liturgical insight. Uniquely for its time the authorized text included three pages of 'coaching' material, and the final *Patterns for Worship* (1995) and its successor *New Patterns for Worship* (2002) not only had sample texts in a variety of resource sections, but also expanded commentary material (with three churches getting it right in a variety of contexts, and one, St Dodo's, getting it wrong). The onus was placed wholly on the individual worshipping group or church to take decisions, shape an act of worship and then find liturgical and teaching material which would make it both locally appropriate and also clearly linked to the Church of England and the Church as a whole.

A Service of the Word after twenty years

After its four-year incubation period, *Patterns for Worship* and A Service of the Word were formally approved and released to the Church of England in 1993. A consideration of their effect and influence will range from facts which are verifiable to impressions which are wholly subjective. A judgement of any measure of 'success' is perhaps beyond the remit of a single author. Nevertheless, *Patterns* set itself some specific challenges and targets, and something can be said about these. The liturgical world view of the late 1980s is, however, radically different from the context of 2011, and a final question must therefore be asked as to whether A Service of the

Word remains fit for purpose in the age of Twitter and Messy Church.

Frameworks for freedom

It is undeniable that since its own authorization A Service of the Word has been remarkably useful in saving vast amounts of time creating new liturgies for the Church of England. Any new service of Morning or Evening Prayer can by-pass the normal 22-stage process for new liturgy which is alternative to the Book of Common Prayer simply by being shown to conform to the provisions of A Service of the Word. This is the case for the services of Morning and Evening Prayer for Sundays printed in the *Common Worship* main volume, and for the whole of *Common Worship: Daily Prayer* (2005), where the authorization page says that 'the orders for Prayer During the Day, Morning and Evening Prayer and Night Prayer comply with the provisions of A Service of the Word'.[16] This has enabled a much more flexible approach to the creation of new 'official' liturgy for the Church of England. The team producing *Daily Prayer* were able to produce an entire volume which was legal, send a provisional edition around the whole Church, and give the greatest opportunity for response before producing the work in a final form.

This also means that revision of such 'word' services is much easier to contemplate, meaning only the practicalities of a new publication rather than the overly complicated revision processes of other authorized liturgy. There are, however, some negative factors to take into account. Some people take great comfort in knowing that a liturgical text has been thoroughly worked over by the relevant bodies, with a thorough revision process at each stage. By contrast these 'pre-authorized' liturgies can often have a very quick passage through the Synod, with a restricted opportunity for the wider Church to have its say. In addition, *Common Worship: Daily Prayer* may have been produced with the involvement of the central structures of the Church of England, but in the end it is only *a* form of daily prayer for the Church of England, not *the* form. Though fully authorized, it is more obviously provisional than its predecessors, only an example and not the 'required' text. In this way some feel that the sense and form of 'common' prayer is further diluted.

The authorization of a permissive and intentionally flexible liturgy has also been successful in bringing in forms of prayer from other traditions and retrospectively recognizing them as authorized forms of prayer for the Church of England. *Celebrating Common Prayer*, originally from the Franciscan tradition, broadly conforms to the requirements of A Service of the Word. Patterns from Iona, the Northumbria Community, and from other denominations can all now be used in great confidence (and with just a little tinkering), and can be claimed as examples of the breadth of Anglican worship. Again, this success has its challenges for those who value a sense of commonality among Anglicans, though the drawing of riches and wisdom from other traditions is perhaps a greater strength.

Further, the authorization of the structure of A Service of the Word has enabled those who produce resources for Sunday worship to create liturgies which combine a robust structure with creative elements and imaginative applications. The Liturgical Commission contributed to this by offering a huge range of texts for different parts of the service, and also by providing 'sample services' in *New Patterns for Worship*. Not only are there services for the 'inherited' liturgical year, there are also forms for the 'secular' calendar, with services for Father's Day and Valentine's Day, among others. This encouragement has been taken up by various authors and publishers, most notably Kevin Mayhew, whose range includes books like *Freedom within a Framework*[17] which take the principles and the strictures of A Service of the Word and put creative flesh upon them. Where the 'official texts' are light on 'action' (which the Commission recognized at the outset), many of these resources fill the gap.

What is clear is that, by recognizing the movement towards 'all-age' worship, and giving it structure and resources, *Patterns for Worship* and A Service of the Word have enabled a remarkable flourishing of liturgical creativity, and given depth and breadth to forms of worship which were in danger of being detached from the rest of the liturgical life of the Church of England. Examples I have seen across the Diocese of York exemplify the usefulness of having some required elements and then pointers to actions and further resources. The basic structure has enabled an amazing variety of forms, far beyond the familiar morning 'family' service originally envisaged. One incumbent supplied me with six different frameworks, ranging from all-age worship, to Morning Prayer in seasonal time, to two diocesan festivals of music and worship. A Service of the Word has become the essential place to start, either for those planning worship in the local context, or for publishers and groups offering resources for them.

All targets met?

A Service of the Word introduced a new way of creating and enacting worship to the Church of England as a whole. To start with the structure of a service, taking into account factors including the season, the geographical and cultural context and the nature of the congregation, followed only then by the selection of texts, and taking into account the 'flow' of the service as well as giving the opportunity for action and response, is now much more the practice of local congregations and churches than it was in 1989. It forms the basis of much of the teaching about worship-leading and -planning across dioceses, and on lay and ordained training courses. An interesting 'official' example is 'The Outline Order for Funerals' in *Common Worship: Pastoral Services*.[18] Though the twelve headings are presented in one fixed order, the page owes everything to A Service of the Word. An introduction could almost say: 'Here are the headings. Some of these sections require authorized texts, otherwise you are free to use any suitable material. Now make it work for each different situation.'

Even if parochial church councils (PCCs) have not taken a formal decision to use A Service of the Word as the authorization for their non-eucharistic worship, it is that service which provides the underpinning and rationale of much of the variety of worship of the Church today. I would venture that the Liturgical Commission's hopes that types of worship which looked as if they might break free from the 'mainstream' of Anglican worship have not only been kept in but have indeed been deepened themselves and have enriched the rest of our Church's worship. Much was made at the time of the notion of 'family likeness': that we would recognize each other not by our slavish adherence to uniform texts, but in shared patterns and traditions. A Service of the Word has given this hope the best possible form, and I have delighted on occasions in telling churches which have generally prided themselves on being un-Anglican actually how Anglican they are now being. The structure and material are pretty robust, and the Church of England liturgical family will only break apart completely if our training and reflection on worship is poorly resourced and applied. The tools are there and have been found to be fit for their purpose.

Not everything envisaged by *Patterns* came to pass. The original *Patterns* had hoped that there would be a 'Rite C' Holy Communion, fully usable as a main act of worship on a Sunday, with all the flexibility of the 'Word' service, and with Eucharistic Prayers which reflected the spirit of this locally appropriate material. Such a Eucharist would meet the needs of the urban and of the Family Service, and would recognize the presence of many children (though it fought shy of a specific Eucharistic Prayer for this purpose). It was not to be, and at final author-ization what remained was A Service of the Word with a Celebration of Holy Communion: spectacularly flexible but 'not normally to be used as the regular Sunday or weekday service'. While the development of A Service of the Word from the original *Patterns* to final authorization in 1999 was one of increasing flexibility, the Eucharist was, to an extent, tightened, and any flexibility greatly constrained. Only in 2011, for example, will further Eucharistic Prayers for use when children are present come before the Synod.

Patterns also hoped that such an approach to liturgy in the Church of England would become 'obviously part of the liturgy of the whole church'.[19] Given that many of its principles are now at the centre of liturgical teaching and practice, it is profoundly puzzling that *New Patterns for Worship* is not part of the *Common Worship* 'brand'. Though A Service of the Word is in 'pole position' at the beginning of the *Common Worship* main volume, *New Patterns* has not been re-titled *Common Worship: Patterns for Worship*, and some have accused the Liturgical Commission and the Church generally of relegating it to the status of a book for those who 'like to do that kind of thing', and not as being 'proper' liturgy. The divide is seen most clearly in the difference between the seasonal material in *Common Worship: Times and Seasons* and *New Patterns*. Many texts are shared, but *Times and Seasons* has much more of an 'official' feel. It may be advantageous to have a volume which is more obviously 'risky', but the perception that it is looked down upon is hard to shift, and might perhaps be a disappointment to those who framed the original *Patterns* two decades ago.

Challenges for the future

Patterns for Worship opened up possibilities for creative and flexible liturgies which, as noted above, many publishers have taken with both hands. Not all their offerings can however be contained even within the flexible provisions of A Service of the Word. Many of them take advantage of the use of a common lectionary across the denominations and provide material for the wider Church which needs to be adapted in order to meet the Church of England's requirements, and the great temptation is to go with what is offered by the publisher rather than tweak the texts. Specific difficulties apply to the Prayers of Penitence and the Affirmation of Faith. Much of what is on offer either has no such material, or uses texts which are not authorized. If the service is a 'main' one then authorized texts are required. But the principle of a flexible and context-dependent liturgy, meeting local needs and encouraging local creativity, is now so deeply embedded that I am sure that this requirement is being overwhelmed or ignored. This is not restricted to all-age services. A traditional service of nine lessons and carols held on a Sunday fails to comply with A Service of the Word as it omits these two sections. At York Minster we had the bizarre experience of having to say a fully legal Evensong with three people in a side chapel, while some thousands waited patiently in the nave for a service which, par excellence, was to engage with the Word and the story of redemption.

A revision of A Service of the Word might well have to look at the requirements of these sections. Underneath this might be a deeper challenge as to why the Church of England requires Prayers of Penitence in all its main services, and, if we do, whether such prayers must all be authorized. A middle way through this might then be an increasing provision of well worked examples of Kyrie confessions, which are legal and allow for greater flexibility and freedom. Affirmations of Faith bring greater complexities, as the need for a corporate recital of the essentials of the faith is hard to argue against. But the most creative of services can be brought up short by a reasonably formal use of a Creed or Affirmation. The provision of one authorized sung creed is a pointer to future developments. Many congregations took this as a hint and included other 'credal' songs and hymns in their repertoire, none of which is authorized. If authorization is important then there will need to be a review of the choices of texts which are offered.

Despite this, A Service of the Word has proved remarkably durable, and capable of adapting to circumstances which the original compilers might not have imagined. The 'directory' approach is much easier to sustain and resource in the age of the internet. The 'structure' approach is tailor made for the era of electronic communication and design. The creation of tailored orders is second nature for even the smallest of worshipping communities, where local printing or projection are now the norm rather than the exception. The principles, elaborated in *Patterns*, that worship should be for all and include all, and could be Anglican even so, have been shown to be prescient and prophetic. It will be interesting to see how A Service of the Word adapts to movements like Godly Play and Messy Church: it will not take much to apply the underlying commitment to structure and family likeness to these and to any future developments. The door, opened by the *ASB* and widened by *Patterns*, is now firmly opened in *Common Worship*. A Service of the Word got it right. Perhaps the greatest measure of its success is that many people who are using it don't know that they are.

Notes

1 Trevor Lloyd, Jane Sinclair and Michael Vasey, *Introducing Patterns for Worship*, Grove Worship Series 111, Bramcote, Grove Books, 1990, p. 4. <www.grovebooks.co.uk>

2 The 'Prefatory Note' to *Patterns for Worship* says that the House of Bishops asked for a 'handbook(s)' which aimed 'to indicate where advantage might be taken of notes and rubrics in the *ASB* to develop and enrich the liturgy'. *Patterns for Worship*, London, Church House Publishing, 1989, p. v.

3 *Patterns for Worship*, p. v.

4 *Patterns for Worship*, p. 1.

5 *Patterns for Worship*, p. 2.

6 Trevor Lloyd, *A Service of the Word*, Grove Worship Series 151, Cambridge, Grove Books, 1999, p. 6.

7 See Paul Bradshaw (ed.), *A Companion to Common Worship*, vol. 1, London, SPCK, 2001, pp. 54ff. for a fuller picture of this development.

8 Lloyd, *A Service of the Word*, p. 5.

9 Noted in Bradshaw, *A Companion to Common Worship*, p. 59.

10 *Patterns for Worship*, p. 3.

11 *Patterns for Worship*, p. 5. The last bullet point was illustrated by a quotation from a four-year-old who said: 'Now I know churches are true: the people in them enjoy singing and moving about in patterns.' I have wondered occasionally who collected this quotation. It may have been David Stancliffe, who certainly knew it by heart and wrote it out for me once when I didn't have the book to hand.

12 *Patterns for Worship*, p. 8.

13 *Patterns for Worship*, p. 21.

14 *Patterns for Worship*, p. 22.
15 A Service of the Word (1999), in *Common Worship: Services and Prayers for the Church of England*, London, Church House Publishing, 2000. Further extracts from A Service of the Word are taken from this volume.
16 *Common Worship: Daily Prayer*, London, Church House Publishing, 2005.
17 Tim Lomax, *Freedom within a Framework* (2001) and *More Freedom within a Framework* (2002), Stowmarket, Kevin Mayhew Publishing.
18 *Common Worship: Pastoral Services*, London, Church House Publishing, 2005.
19 *Patterns for Worship*, p. 2.

Part 2

COMMON WORSHIP: BRINGING THE LITURGY TO LIFE

5

Believing in a God who sings

SIMON REYNOLDS

———◆•◆•◆———

Je crois en Dieu qui chante
Et qui fait chanter la vie.[1]

Over the past couple of decades, the Church has invested
heavily in programmes and processes which seek to nurture
people in the faith. Behind their various brand identities is a
foundational (and sometimes non-negotiable) assumption that
Christian formation is largely contingent upon a systematic,
didactic encounter with the Church's biblical and dogmatic
categories. Those which encompass a liturgical, or even musical,
dimension do so as a secondary, lifestyle-focused consideration.
This is a curious (and questionable) stance for those who aspire
to offer a distinctively *Anglican* mode of evangelization. As one
commentator has asked: is Thomas Cranmer, as the architect of
the Book of Common Prayer, the definitive Anglican systematic
theologian, precisely because his liturgical work seeks to 'make
Christian theology and Christian practice interdependent in a
Christian *praxis*'?[2]

It seems reasonable to ask, ten years after the publication
of *Common Worship*, whether the music which surrounds liturgical celebration can become a primary vehicle of formation
and transformation. Can people absorb the gospel and articulate the faith of the Church as effectively through song as
through statement? Do we have sufficient confidence in the
capacity of liturgical music to engage those who seek wellsprings
of meaning and cohesion for their lives – particularly where
that music may demand a significant degree of cultural,

intellectual and spiritual attention from those who hear it or perform it? How might those responsible for ordering worship employ a greater degree of theological rigour and cultural imagination in the musical choices they make? And how might those choices enable worshippers to glimpse the reality of divine 'otherness' as well as the possibility of a transformed world?

An implicit creed: the experience of cathedrals

Patrick Gale's novel *The Whole Day Through* describes twenty-four hours in the life of Laura Lewis. After enjoying romantic independence in Paris for some years, she returns to Britain to look after her ageing mother in Winchester. As the afternoon draws on, Laura drives her mother to the cathedral for Evensong.

> Creed aside, it was a wonderfully undemanding ritual, almost a concert. The music varied hugely, from sparse polyphonic and plainchant settings used on nights when only mens' voices were available through lush Victorian settings and turn of the century tearjerkers to challenging contemporary ones. There was no tedious sermon, no tub-thumping hymn. After several exposures, Laura found she was enjoying the psalms, with their frequent bouts of despair or indignation, and the unexpected charm of the readings. Much of it meant nothing to her but she still found she could appreciate it . . . The words, especially those of the nunc dimittis and the repeated references to night and stillness . . . the inevitable identification of the end of the day with the end of life, tended to bring on a curious fit of nostalgia or species of homesickness, a dwelling on chances past and friends lost, that could make her tearful if she didn't guard against it.[3]

Those who work in many of the Church of England's cathedrals will immediately recognize Laura as a frequent and familiar presence at Evensong, or possibly the Sunday Eucharist. They will also know that, as the past couple of decades have witnessed the voluble promotion of programmes of nurture and evangelism, the Church of England's cathedrals (and other choral foundations) have been quietly enjoying something of a renaissance.[4] Current evidence suggests that attendance at worship has risen significantly, and that they attract worshippers of a greater age-range than might typically be found worshipping in a parish church.[5] They attract because they tend to offer a distinctive spatial environment, anonymity, a higher standard of preaching, liturgical creativity and, most significantly, musical excellence. Deans and Chapters justifiably insist that the huge annual music budget is a major element of the overall missionary enterprise. The dynamics of choral worship, coupled to the ambience of the building in which it takes place, can function as a conduit between aesthetic pleasure and religious attachment.

Grace Davie has suggested that music in cathedrals functions as a 'language' which enables hearers to slip back and forth between the aesthetic and the religious. Citing Mozart and Bach as examples of the way this language bridges different worlds, Davie highlights the interchangeability of identical themes and motifs in their sacred and secular works:

> The theme was first and foremost an inspired 'geste musical' – its appropriation by either religion or the theatre was secondary. The musical settings of the Mass or the Passion contain similar ambiguities; it is not necessary to be a Christian to appreciate both their musical and dramatic power.[6]

Cathedrals are often spoken of as places of 'cultural curiosity' where, as Davie has repeatedly suggested, the growth in attendance at worship has coincided with an increase in the numbers undertaking pilgrimages across Europe.[7] Often the liturgy is stumbled upon, and music can be a persuasive dimension in enabling seekers and enquirers to feel their way into the rituals and beliefs of the Church. There is less pressure to join in or sign up; and (like charismatic Evangelical congregations, which represent the other focus of growth in recent years) cathedrals and their music offer 'an experience' which appeals to the present cultural preference for consumption over commitment.

Consequently, those who order worship and direct music within cathedrals and larger churches must discern how an initial cultural curiosity can become more than a desire for mere entertainment. This is especially germane when account is taken of the influence of Classic FM, for example, and the growth in consumption of classical music as a recreational activity.

One particular way of facing this challenge is emerging in the attempts by some cathedrals and large city centre churches to offer 'alternative' acts of worship (usually late in the evening) in addition to the traditional choral provision. York Minster's 'Transcendence – An Ancient Future Mass' and Wakefield's 'Missa' are just two examples of how 'blended' or 'synthesis' worship (where a range of contemporary music styles are combined with a traditional liturgical framework) is gaining a place alongside Choral Evensong. Specifically aimed at Generation Y, these services seek to offer a distinctive post-modern form of worship for those who have not been nurtured in a church environment, but who are open to a spiritual dimension and enjoy a range of contemporary music styles beyond the 'soft folk' idiom of many worship songs used in established Evangelical churches. Some commentators have observed how these emerging forms of worship place a great deal of emphasis not only on more recent contemporary music styles (rock, rap, garage, etc.), but also employ more primitive music such as chant and organum.[8] The result is considerably more than a 'rave in the nave' or a rock concert which just happens to take place in a large church. A recent survey highlights the degree to which such services are liturgically structured, with a particular emphasis on eucharistic hospitality; an implied scriptural orthodoxy (aided by a regard for the lectionary); an interest in recovering more ancient and complex liturgical forms; a suspicion of hierarchy and the encouragement of participation by all; an emphasis on the rhythm of the liturgical year and the seasons; and an acceptance of diversity.[9] Current evidence suggests that this form of liturgy is proving just as effective in nurturing worshippers, and in enabling them to engage with Scripture and tradition, as the traditional choral provision in our cathedrals.

Words and music: learning a new language

It is significant that the growth being experienced by cathedrals is the culmination of repeated and imaginative responses to the changing social and cultural contours of recent decades. No longer can they be caricatured as places of refuge for those sheltering from recent liturgical developments. With the exception of daily Choral Evensong, where the Book of Common Prayer remains the staple diet, cathedrals have demonstrated a dexterous capacity to cultivate the *Common Worship* rites as part of their distinctive liturgical topography. Similarly, there has been a consistent endeavour by the musicians who work in cathedrals to 'raise the game' to the extent that, on the whole, the music which envelops cathedral liturgy poses a substantial challenge to anyone in search of the anaesthetizing effects of 'muzak'. Allan Wicks at Canterbury (1961–88), Stephen Cleobury at King's College, Cambridge (1982–), Martin Neary at Winchester (1971–86), and John Scott at St Paul's (1991–2004) are four names which exemplify the late twentieth- and early twenty-first-century drive to purge the cathedral repertoire of the saccharine and sub-standard, and to encourage mainstream contemporary composers to write serious works for liturgical use which make few – if any – artistic compromises.[10] Anyone attending choral worship in cathedrals today should expect to encounter not only the exigent language of contemporary music or the primitive unison of plainsong, but also the contrapuntal complexities of renaissance polyphony or the harmonic sophistication of the baroque period. Moreover, this music, whatever its age, is no longer heard 'speaking' with an English accent, as contemporary works from the former Eastern bloc, seventeenth-century Mexico or nineteenth-century Europe – invariably sung in their original languages – are heard alongside works by British composers. It bears witness to a creative catholicity, and goes some way towards undermining the superficial perception that choral worship is culturally exclusive.

From cathedral to parish: music and the other

This development is significant, not only for the renewal of cathedral worship, but also in offering a pattern for parishes and other worshipping communities which do not enjoy the professional musical resources of our choral foundations. It challenges a propensity to be musically and liturgically hidebound, and should encourage the cultivation of a more diverse musical palette than is currently the case. If one of the primary goals of liturgical celebration is a desire to enable the people of God to engage in a reciprocal conversation with the triune God,[11] it is entirely reasonable to expect that the 'language' of that conversation will be, by degrees, as strange and unfamiliar as it will be recognizable and recurring; and the choice of liturgical music should similarly reflect this reality. Questioning the default preference for a familiar idiom in church music, the contemporary English composer Michael Berkeley asks:

> Do contemporary composers feel that church music requires a degree of compromise, making it inevitable that sacred music becomes a musically conservative landscape, the preserve of composers who specialise in performable and 'accessible' music? Perhaps. But Byrd, Victoria, Palestrina, Bach and Mozart did not feel the need to shackle their creativity when tackling sacred commissions. Why is it that today we settle for something that often fails to rise above the anodyne?[12]

Berkeley's concern is that the Church has been content to collude with a situation where the gap between artistic originality and a primary desire for practical accessibility is widening. He challenges liturgists, musicians and educationalists to overcome the rising dependence on the familiar – or, more specifically, the tonal – sound world of church music. Writing of his recent experience of composing for the liturgy, Berkeley writes:

I became conscious of other, practical problems facing church music: the familiarity of tonality (the major and minor scale . . .) and the standard of singing in most choirs . . . The long-term solution here lies in education and exposing young children to a much wider musical landscape than the one they are offered now. We would then not have the problem with tonality, or lack of it . . . The tonal problem has arisen because our ears, and therefore our voices, tend to feel at home with major and minor scales and the intervals that they produce. We can all sing the interval C to F, for instance: we do so every time we sing 'Away in a Manger'. But what about C to F sharp?[13]

Transcendence and immanence

This appeal for a more daring musical creativity points to a fundamental theological consideration which ought to under-pin the ordering of the liturgy and the choice of music as much in parishes as in cathedrals. If one of the principal intentions of the Church's worship is an invitation to glimpse something of the otherness of God, to be (in Frank Senn's words) enchanted rather than entertained,[14] and to be confronted by the strange-ness of the divine presence, to what degree is the language, the symbolism and the music employed in worship facilitating or hindering this purpose?

The insights of the twentieth-century liturgical movement, as well as the reforms of the Second Vatican Council, which led to a necessary rediscovery of the communitarian dimension of liturgical celebration, has also resulted in a liturgical climate where divine immanence, and accessibility of meaning, is the principal emphasis in many worshipping communities. Perhaps after a decade of worshipping with the new rites in the Church of England, this is an appropriate moment to take stock and ask whether the balance needs to be redressed. Do those who order the Church's worship feel sufficiently confident in challenging a demand for immediate accessibility in a culture of instant gratification; or is there too much pressure (in the name of a one-dimensional view of 'mission') to prize the effortless or the informal as the favoured musical and liturgical perspective?

In a consumerist culture, where God easily becomes just another commodity in a world of non-stop choice, is there an emerging nervousness about signifying that liturgical participation might properly make intellectual and cultural demands on worshippers; and that the 'language' of worship (especially its musical element) needs to be not only learnt, but repeatedly worked at and discovered afresh?

The biblical witness, as much as the Church's theological and spiritual tradition, is cautious of effortless epiphanies, as two examples from the twentieth century might usefully highlight. Rudolf Otto's renowned suggestion, that God is a tremendous mystery which fascinates and attracts,[15] is developed by Hans Urs von Balthasar's writing on theological aesthetics.[16] The latter's suggestion that God is revealed as beauty, and that the outward form of beauty will in-form the worshipper and impress its mark upon the life of the worshipper, is mirrored by the suggestion that the more we comprehend God's self-revelation the more we are aware of God's self-concealment. Whatever we may know about God, there are mysteries beyond our perception which necessitate further searching, as we are invited to respond to a vision which fascinates and inspires greater discernment of the divine truth and beauty.

These are just two potentially fruitful insights which might underpin the choices made by those who order worship and choose the musical elements within it. It is to be hoped they will also sound a note of caution to those who seem too eager, in their liturgical and musical choices, to short-circuit the time and perseverance that are a necessary element in the search fully to comprehend the divine presence at work – and at play – in creation.

Whose song are we singing?

This may reasonably give rise to the question of whether, in our evolving use of the new liturgical rites, we are merely content to suggest that we believe in a God who only sings *our* songs; or do our encounters with the divine reality induce a longing to discover a 'new song' that is unexpected or unknown, but which may become a natural part of our worshipping vocabulary? Where there is a willingness to persist with a vision of divine otherness, it can impart a sense of ontological homecoming:

> Writers in the past have told how violently they reacted to their first encounter with the music of Stravinsky, or in the nineteenth century with the paintings of Cézanne, or in the eighteenth with the wildness of the Alps, only to be drawn back by the very power they had perceived and rejected and find it beautiful beyond their imagining ... When music speaks wordlessly like an illumination, people know they are receiving, not imposing, its meaning ... The music comes out to meet them and address them as an 'other', and nothing can persuade them that they are looking merely at their own feelings reflected in a mirror.[17]

Words and music: wrestling with meaning

It is notable that the process of liturgical revision in the 1960s and 1970s, which resulted in the *Alternative Service Book*, as well as the translation of the post-conciliar *Roman Missal*, took place in parallel with the drive for 'functional equivalence' in biblical translation (of which the *Good News Bible* is, perhaps, the iconic exemplar).[18] A brief backward glance reveals an environment in which clarity of meaning was prized above rhythm, allusion, metaphor, or tracing the poetic contours of texts. We were supposed to grasp 'what it means' on first encounter. The shortcomings of this approach were soon seized upon by cultural commentators, social psychologists, poets and composers – as well as being frequently parodied by satirists!

A later generation of liturgists has recognized that texts need to be written with an underlying rhythm and with a view to being sung. There has been a discernible move away from composing liturgical texts as step-by-step instruction manuals, to imagining their use as one element in a sacred performance, where speech, action, music, silence, smell and colour communicate at different but equally valid levels.[19]

This should be seen as much more than a preference for cultural superiority in the liturgy. Social anthropologists have identified the value of small-scale, repetitive techniques which enable people to assess their perceptions, examine their unconscious longings, or consider the formation of motive. The value of this in relation to the performance of liturgy and the appropriation of new music might be that, by being given time and space to work at it, we are bringing an 'external mind' to bear. As Timothy Jenkins has suggested, such recurring activity

> represents the possibility, and . . . the truth, that we are not simply the sum of our egos and strivings, but are capable of extraordinarily more, and indeed are ordered quite differently . . . the key to our lives is gift, not equivalence or calculation.[20]

Similar notions can be detected in the so-called 'Mozart Effect'. Several studies into the cognitive effects of Mozart's music have identified its capacity to increase spatial-temporal reasoning. This is, admittedly, a controversial area of neurological research, but some studies have discovered that listening to complex music actually excites the cortical firing patterns that are analogous to those used in spatial reasoning.[21] Experiments to measure psychological parameters in the brain, conducted among patients with neurological disorders, revealed that Mozart's music had the capacity to stabilize the agitation associated with such conditions.[22] Those who have studied the Mozart Effect believe it is accounted for because no other composer (except J. S. Bach) employs the repetition of shapes and contours of musical phrases with the same degree of symmetry, variation and patterning.

A counter-insight reveals the capacity of plainsong to function at a different level in counteracting the constraints of time. With its distinctive patterning, it has proved especially effective in palliative care, because of the absence of bar lines and time signatures, which creates a sense of timelessness and evocation of eternity. Its importance in ministering to a dying person was memorably expressed by a priest who used the *Kyrie* from the plainsong *Missa de Angelis*.[23]

Particular examples of contemporary composers whose liturgical music reflects this patterned and repetitive idiom include the Scottish Catholic James MacMillan (whose symphonic and operatic works are an established part of the 'secular' repertoire). He produces new liturgical music on an almost weekly basis for the inner-city church in Glasgow where he directs the music. His published works for 'parish use' such as the *Galloway Mass* and *St Anne Mass*[24] reveal his capacity to write for limited resources (an organist or pianist capable of playing a four-part hymn tune will quickly master the accompaniment) while making few artistic compromises over rhythmic and harmonic complexity. Colin Mawby (another Roman Catholic composer who writes for sacred and secular contexts) has just completed a three-year cycle of responsorial psalmody for the Principal Service lectionary, which offers a fresh approach to a genre that has become tired by being predictably wedded to the oft-appropriated scheme devised by Dom Gregory Murray in the 1960s.[25] The responsorial eucharistic acclamations by Huw Williams, written for the Sunday Eucharist at St Paul's Cathedral, have been designed to be grasped by congregations predominated by once-only worshippers of different nationalities, which incorporate harmonic interest for a choir.[26] John Tavener has composed a setting of the Lord's Prayer[27] where the congregation may simply sing the text on one note, and the choir (or organ) is given simple but striking harmony in 'step-by-step' movement which provides an ethereal effect. Tavener, like his contemporary Arvo Pärt, creates a timelessness in his music through repetition, and absorbing influences from various Eastern Orthodox traditions; whereas the Catholic Pärt has spoken of creating a fresh and unexpected soundworld from as little as possible:

> I have discovered that it is enough when a single note is beautifully played. This one note, or a silent beat, or a moment of silence, comforts me. I work with very few elements – with one voice, with two voices. I build with the most primitive materials . . .[28]

Hymnody: an expanse of belief in song

In a previous post, one of my responsibilities involved the weekly selection of 16 hymns to be sung at the regular Sunday and weekday services. The majority who attended those services were once-only visitors, whose first language may not have been English, who had no previous experience of Anglican choral worship, and whose religious tradition may even have been non-Christian. Alongside these visitors there would have been a smattering of 'regulars' as well as aficionados of choral worship from elsewhere. It was always a delicate balancing act. In addition to the obvious criteria for choosing hymns (reflecting the readings, season or theme, using tunes that echoed the general style of music in the service, providing metrical and musical variety over the course of a week, and so forth), I was aware of the need to provide hymns that might evoke a recognizable soundscape for international visitors (for example the recurring use of half a dozen or so plainsong tunes such as *Veni Creator Spiritus* or *Te lucis ante terminum*; and occasional Lutheran chorales or Genevan Psalter melodies such as 'Eisenach' or 'Rendez à Dieu'). These would punctuate a diet of hymns whose words and tunes might be more familiar to an English-speaking Anglican, as well as the inclusion of more recent material from hymn-books published by different Christian denominations in the past 25 years.[29] A further challenge was posed by the need to ensure that the words exposed worshippers (especially those whose attendance was more regular), over each period or season, to a fully synoptic and engaging account of the Christian faith. Nonetheless, I would still receive frequent pleas to include more 'well-known' hymns!

One of the obvious musical consequences of the contracting place of religion in the public sphere is that the majority of Generations X and Y have grown up without exposure to a basic diet of Christian hymnody as part of collective worship in school. Equally, the proliferation of hymn-books in the past 20 years, many with a 'party' slant, has contributed to an ever-decreasing 'pool' of words and music which Christians have in common. More significantly, a situation is emerging in which regular worshippers are being exposed to a more restricted diet of language, history and theology in the words (and sometimes the music) they sing. In many congregations, some of the classic hymns which characterize the principal festivals of the Christian year, or which articulate some of the principal themes of Christian belief, either are unknown or have been displaced by something less enduring.

A contracting vision?

Hymns (and worship songs) provide the principal opportunity for worshippers to be exposed to – and encouraged to explore – an ever-widening landscape of credal Christianity, and to grasp something of the nature of divine revelation. Consequently, a greater importance will need to be attached to the choice of hymns, as well as the composition of new texts (and tunes) which take account of the paucity of particular theological themes or seasons of the Christian year (Candlemas, as a pivotal moment in the Christian year, is one obvious example). It is also becoming obvious that worshipping communities will need to invest time and resources in the technology that will reduce their dependence on a single hymn-book, and allow themselves to become more familiar not only with less 'well-known' hymns, but also an ever-developing repertoire as new material becomes available. Anglicans, unlike our Methodist counterparts, have been rather coy about recognizing the value of hymns as a resource for formation; and, at worst, regard them merely as convenient liturgical staging-posts. Environmental concerns, which make the production of detailed weekly service sheets increasingly indefensible, could, in a short space of time, be succeeded by pre-programmed, hand-held electronic devices which will immediately multiply the musical and literary repertoire available for a congregation. At the present moment, however, some notable gaps in the range of hymnody Anglicans use could be profitably addressed. For instance, most Anglican worshippers know barely a handful of the vast output of John and Charles Wesley. Greater familiarity with Methodist hymnals[30] will open up an inexplicably neglected resource, revealing how the Wesleys' work is saturated in not only the language and symbolism of Scripture, but also the writings of the patristic period – a seminal era for the development of Christian belief and identity, rarely given the airing it deserves in preaching, let alone in the composition of liturgical texts.

The value in congregations easing their dependence on a single hymnal is that one book can too often be bound to a particular cultural and theological mindset, with all the potential for inhibiting formation. For example, it is now possible to see that many Anglican hymnals published since the 1980s have a particular theological 'accent' arising from the preponderance of new compositions they contain (and the criteria employed for excluding particular items). While there have been some notably fine and creative examples, much which typifies the 'Hymn Explosion' (with which Fred Kaan, Michael Forster, Brian Wren and Fred Pratt Green are most associated) reflects an anthropocentric, time-specific social spirituality. Many also signal a specific dependence on late nineteenth- and twentieth-century European Protestant theological and philosophical thought.

Similar things could be said of contemporary worship songs. Not only can an allegedly 'modern' musical style soon date when compared to developments in the wider world of 'popular' music, it is also possible to discern an equally myopic theological perspective. A number of commentators[31] have noted the preponderance of recurring themes to the extent that any congregation relying on one collection of worship songs may find that their singing leaves them inhabiting a semi-permanent Passiontide undergirded by one particular theology of the atonement. Alongside this emphasis is a reliance on the language and imagery of submission to divine power and omnipotence, and the holiness of the individual worshipper. Few (if any) references can be found to the incarnation and ministry of Jesus, divine passibility in the passion, or the divine response to human injustice and suffering.

The American Methodist scholar Lester Ruth has undertaken a survey of 72 of the most popular contemporary worship
songs, and has identified a clear Trinitarian imbalance.[32] Of
those surveyed, only three meet the criteria of naming the
Trinity, directing a congregation's worship and prayer towards
the Trinity, or evoking something of the character of the Trinity
and how worshippers may participate in the life of the Trinity.
Of those three, the *refrain* to Graham Kendrick's 'Shine, Jesus,
shine' passes muster! Ruth's contention is that this arises from
a low expectation, by those who compose and sing these songs,
that worship needs to express or scrutinize the corporate faith
of the Church. Instead the emphasis is most often placed on
the cultivation of a personal relationship with God (aided by
the language of intimacy). This suggests, at the very least, an
imbalance of reason in relation to revelation.

Contemporary hymn-writing which does imaginatively
address the inadequacies already identified can be found in
some of the work of the Iona Community (especially the work
of John Bell and Graham Maule). Deserving of much wider
consideration is a collection, containing many vivid hymns which
address hitherto neglected themes and seasons of the year, by
Rosalind Brown, Jeremy Davies and Ron Green.[33] Although it
was published in 1996, few worshipping communities have
explored the potential of *Hymns for Prayer and Praise*, which
contains many vibrant translations of early medieval hymns,
as well as new texts and (*quasi*-plainsong) tunes from monastic
communities, which would certainly meet the needs of congregations with limited musical resources.[34]

A God who sings

It is becoming commonplace in the Church of England to speak
about a 'mixed economy' approach to music in worship, and
that is just a hint of what Anglicanism has always aimed to be.
However, as our understanding of the nature of Christian faith
is defined, to a large extent, by the way we worship, it is crucial
that this approach should not indicate a preference for style

over substance. Music has a unique capacity to point beyond self, beyond the sameness of many people's daily grind, beyond our limited expectations, to the indefinable and transforming reality of God. Those of us who are afforded the privilege of ordering the Church's worship are charged with the responsibility of ensuring that the words and music of the liturgy will excite, challenge and inspire a vision of beauty and hopefulness that speaks most truly about ourselves and the God in whose image we are created.

The history and practice of Christian worship bears witness to a dynamic evolution of language, symbols and music. These elements reflect the Church's evolving vision of Jesus Christ as the living Word of God in different times and cultures. That same history has also revealed that, when the Church has sought to define that vision solely by a written code, and reduced liturgical celebration to words on a page, something vital has been lost. Christian belief and Christian living are drawn together in the dynamic encounter of heaven and earth, human and divine. It is the active speech and the living song of the body of Christ which gives substance to our hope, and enables us to proclaim the faith afresh in every generation. When the Church is liberated to sing a new song, the celebration of the liturgy can become the lively and energetic arena of Christian formation it is meant to be.

In a startling, yet salutary, reminder from a poet who was ambivalent about Christian faith, the source of all our believing, worshipping and living cannot be locked between the covers of a book, but lives – and sings!

> Who is this that comes in splendour, coming from the blazing East?
> This is he we had not thought of, this is he the airy Christ.
> Airy, in an airy manner in an airy parkland walking,
> Others take him by the hand, lead him, do the talking.
> But the Form, the airy One, frowns an airy frown,
> What they say he knows must be, but he looks aloofly down,
> Looks aloofly at his feet, looks aloofly at his hands,
> Knows they must, as prophets say, nailèd be to wooden bands.

As he knows the words he sings, that he sings so happily
Must be changed to working laws, yet sings he ceaselessly.
Those who truly hear the voice, the words, the happy song,
Never shall need working laws to keep from doing wrong.
Deaf men will pretend sometimes they hear the song, the words,
And make excuse to sin extremely; this will be absurd.
Heed it not. Whatever foolish men may do the song is cried
For those who hear, and the sweet singer does not care that he
was crucified.
For he does not wish that men should love him more than
anything
Because he died; he only wishes they would hear him sing.[35]

Notes

1 From a hymn by Noel Colombier (I believe in God who sings / and who makes life itself to sing), translation by Paul Iles.

2 W. Taylor Stevenson, 'Lex Orandi—Lex Credendi', in Stephen Sykes, John Booty and Jonathan Knight (eds), *The Study of Anglicanism* (1988), rev. edn, London, SPCK, 1998, p. 188.

3 Patrick Gale, *The Whole Day Through*, London, Fourth Estate, 2009, pp. 157–8. Reprinted by permission of HarperCollins Publishers Ltd © 2009 Patrick Gale.

4 It is significant, for example, that the authors of *Mission-Shaped Church* failed to take sufficient account of the significance of cathedrals as places which offer an 'alternative' to parochial forms of worship.

5 The breakdown of Sunday and weekday attendance at English cathedrals and Westminster Abbey between 1995 and 2009 can be found at <www.cofe.anglican.org/info/statistics/>.

6 Grace Davie, *Religion in Modern Europe: A Memory Mutates*, Oxford, Oxford University Press, 2000, p. 170.

7 Davie, *Religion in Modern Europe*, p. 168; see also Grace Davie, 'A Post-script', in Stephen Platten and Christopher Lewis (eds), *Dreaming Spires?: Cathedrals in a New Age*, London, SPCK, 2006, p. 148.

8 Bryan D. Spinks, *The Worship Mall: Contemporary Responses to Contemporary Culture*, London, SPCK/Alcuin, 2010, pp. 25–30.

9 Michael Perham and Mary Grey-Reeves, *The Hospitality of God*, London, SPCK, 2010.

10 Since 1983, for example, Stephen Cleobury has annually commissioned a new carol from a mainstream contemporary composer for the Festival of Nine Lessons and Carols at King's College, Cambridge (those composed between 1982 and 2004 have been recorded on EMI 5 58070 2); Martin Neary, encouraged by Dean Michael Stancliffe, embarked on a remarkable collaboration with Jonathan Harvey in the late 1970s which resulted in many new works for Winchester which have become an established feature of the contemporary repertoire; and John Scott had a policy of including newly commissioned works for St Paul's Cathedral in the eight-volume *English Anthem* series of recordings (Hyperion Records).

11 An echo of Geoffrey Wainright's description of liturgy as 'a "unique action" in which God and man communicate with one another . . . by means of verbal, material and dramatic signs which were instituted by God through Christ and are now used by the faithful in spiritual obedience'. Cited in Michael Kunzler SJ, *The Church's Liturgy* (English translation), London, Continuum, 2001, p. 5.

12 Michael Berkeley, 'Come Let Us Mumble', *The Guardian*, 21 June 2003.

13 Berkeley, 'Come Let Us Mumble'.

14 Frank C. Senn, *Christian Liturgy: Catholic and Evangelical*, Minneapolis, Fortress, 1977, p. 704.

15 Rudolf Otto's description of God as 'mysterium tremendum et fascinans' was first used in *The Idea of the Holy* (English translation), Oxford, Oxford University Press, 1923.

16 Hans Urs von Balthasar, *The Glory of the Lord*, Edinburgh, T&T Clark, 1991.

17 John V. Taylor, *The Christlike God*, London, SCM Press, 1992, pp. 30–1.

18 For an outline of the principles of this method see for example Eugene A. Nida and Charles R. Tabor, *The Theory and Practice of Translation*, Leiden, Brill, 1969.

19 Along with *Common Worship*, the English translation of the third edition of the *Roman Missal* (which has received the *Recognitio* for use in England and Wales at the time of writing) not only places considerable emphasis on the need for texts to be composed and translated with a view to being sung, but has deliberately moved away from the principle of functional equivalence.

20 Timothy Jenkins, *An Experiment in Providence: How Faith Engages the World*, London, SPCK, 2006, p. 46.

21 Frances Rauscher, Gordon Shaw and K. N. Ky, *Music and Spatial Task Performance: A Casual Relationship*, New York, Nature, especially pp. 365 and 611.

22 Oliver Sacks, *Musicophilia: Tales of Music and the Brain*, London, Picador, 2007.

23 Jeremy Davies, sermon (unpublished) at the annual St Cecilia Festival, St Paul's Cathedral, November 2006.

24 Boosey & Hawkes, 1995 and 1996.

25 At the time of writing, Mawby's settings are unpublished, but enquiries can be made to <www.music-for-church-choirs.com/colin-mawby.html>.

26 Enquiries may be addressed to huwwilliams71@gmail.com.

27 Chester/Novello, 2002.

28 Paul Hillier, 'Arvo Pärt – Magister Ludi', *The Musical Times* 130, no. 1753 (March 1989), pp. 134–7.

29 For example the United Reformed Church's *Rejoice and Sing*, Oxford, Oxford University Press, 1991; *Baptist Praise & Worship*, Oxford, Oxford University Press, 1992; the Church of Scotland's *Church Hymnary* (4th edn), Norwich, Canterbury Press, 2005; and *New English Praise*, Norwich, Canterbury Press, 2006.

30 *Hymns & Psalms* (1983) and *Singing the Faith* (Publication planned for July 2011).

31 See Martyn Percy, *Words, Wonders and Power: Understanding Contemporary Christian Fundamentalism and Revivalism*, London, SPCK, 1996 (esp. pp. 66ff.); and Pete Ward, *Selling Worship: How What We Sing Has Changed the Church*, Bletchley, Paternoster, 2005 (esp. pp. 135ff.).

32 Lester Ruth, 'Lex Amandi, Lex Orandi: The Trinity in the Most-Used Contemporary Christian Worship Songs', in Bryan D. Spinks (ed.), *The Place of Christ in Liturgical Prayer*, Collegeville, Liturgical Press, 2008.

33 Rosalind Brown, Jeremy Davies and Ron Green, *Sing! New Words for Worship*, Salisbury, Sarum College Press, 2004.

34 Panel of Monastic Musicians, *Hymns for Prayer and Praise*, Norwich, Canterbury Press, 1996.

35 Stevie Smith, 'The Airy Christ'.

6

The tent re-pitched

R I C H A R D G I L E S

––––•◦•––––

Eugene O'Neill's play *A Long Day's Journey into Night* is fairly demanding stuff, but for its hauntingly beautiful title alone remains unforgettable. Perhaps we might call the liturgy of Easter 'a long night's journey into day'. Certainly the Easter Vigil itself was originally a journey through the night into the breaking dawn, and if we include the liturgies of the whole of the Triduum (Three Days), then the sense of journey and struggle, the movement from despair and suffering into joy, is all the more manifest.

How might Christian communities today enter into this Paschal journey? How might they do so in such a way that they are not merely observing the Church's rites faithfully, even doggedly, but are drawn deeply into the mystery of Christ, into the paradox at the heart of the gospel, that only through death may we experience life? How might dutiful observance become a life-changing experience of transformation? In other words, how might we rescue the Triduum from the liturgists and give it back to the people of God?

For this to happen we need to understand our participation in these Easter rites as not merely a remembering or facile re-enacting, but rather a risk-taking encounter with the Holy One in which the past is brought shrieking into the present with vivid force. As Dirk Lange makes clear in his book *Trauma Recalled*, the liturgical event is not something that 'can be kept as a memorial ... the event is not an ending, rather it is like a beginning that continually irrupts' in life.[1]

So when we gather for the liturgies of the Three Days we come not to stand and watch from the back of the crowd, but to step forward, risking engagement, putting ourselves in the way of the action as did Simon from Cyrene. He was 'compelled' to carry the cross[2], and we too are compelled by the power of the liturgical action to place ourselves at God's disposal.

As we approach the liturgies of Holy Week and Easter, we should also pause to consider, and give thanks for, the dramatic transformation of these rites in the life of the Church of England. Time was when we were liturgical paupers, gazing through other people's brightly lit windows at the goodies displayed within. Material to enrich the sparse resources of the Book of Common Prayer as far as Holy Week was concerned had to be smuggled over ecclesiastical borders by night. Today, ten years on from *Common Worship* and 26 years after *Lent, Holy Week, Easter* was first published, we find ourselves blessed with resources we could hardly have imagined 40 years ago.

We are rich indeed, and our full, faithful and creative observance of Holy Week and Easter is one of the prime ways of acknowledging and celebrating our new-found wealth.

Numerous factors will determine the degree to which the Easter mysteries come alive for us. Inspired pastoral leadership is always the key element, providing that sense of excitement at the power of liturgy to transform lives. Without such conviction, all attempts to 'brighten up' a received tradition will be like drops of water running into the sand. Good leadership undergirds transformational liturgy at every turn.

Close on the heels of good leadership, however, comes liturgical space. No matter how excellent our liturgical resources, how inspired our pastor, or enthusiastic our faith community, the sacred task of bringing liturgy to life will be hampered at every turn if the room in which we gather is not fit for purpose. If the room speaks of a quite different theological and liturgical framework from that which informs our hearts and minds today, our best efforts at liturgical renewal will be constrained and frustrated. We will be able only to glimpse the possibilities which lie open before us.

Here we come face to face with the immense problems faced by a Church whose building stock is inherited to a large degree from a bygone age. Contemporary worship is enriched by our deeper and more extensive knowledge of our Christian origins, and energized by our access through the web to resources across the globe and by our new-found ability to enhance worship by multi-media technology undreamt of 50 years ago. For most of us, however, we are required to grope towards these fresh insights in rooms laid out by spiritual forebears with a totally different world view and theological understanding. Our new wine may be intoxicating stuff, but only a dribble emerges from the battered and inflexible old wineskins in which the treasure is stored.

Despite the fact that parishes and faith communities through-out the land manfully struggle to stage the liturgies of the Triduum in whatever inherited worship space they find them-selves, we must face up to the reality that the vast majority of these spaces, as presently laid out, are a hindrance rather than an inspiration. Not only are they customarily subdivided into a hierarchical series of rooms distinguished by differences in level and in some cases by screens, low walls, or other barriers, but they are invariably full to the brim with fixed furniture, making it impossible for the assembly to move as a body through the space.

These interiors reduce our notion of liturgical journey to the level of cerebral theory, and this can never be good enough for the pilgrim people of God. At the heart of the Anglican trad-ition of worship is the sacramental principle; that we are called not merely to think about things but to grasp hold of them, not merely to ponder a theory but to actually do the business. The individual person is a unity of body, mind and spirit, and all three need to find expression in our worship. We are not merely thinking people trapped in a body, but whole beings needing food and self-expression in every aspect of our lives.

Any failure to do justice to the whole person in worship, any reduction of liturgical understanding to theory rather than practice, has a particularly devastating effect on the liturgy of

Easter in which living out, not just recalling or contemplating, is of the essence of what we are about. Journey is such a fundamental component of the Triduum experience that to conceptualize it without *doing* it runs the risk of missing the point altogether.

Given the severe constraints of the kind of room we usually find ourselves in when we assemble to do the work of the people of God in liturgy, it is a wonder that Easter means anything more to most Anglicans than daffodils and newborn lambs. Those who strive to produce transformational liturgies in these rigid, unforgiving spaces are heroes of the faith.

So what can be done? Two cathedrals, one on each side of the Atlantic, and each using a very different kind of building, provide models of how inherited spaces, however inadequate in their previous configuration, can be reshaped into rooms fit for liturgical purpose in today's Church.

A consistent voice asserting that the true test of a room set aside for worship is its suitability for the enactment of the Easter liturgy has been that of David Stancliffe, and it is not surprising therefore that the new look of one of these two cathedrals – Portsmouth – was his creation. It was extended and reordered during his time as Provost, in 1991. Its American liturgical cousin is the episcopal, (Anglican) cathedral at Philadelphia, Pennsylvania, reordered in 2002.

Both these buildings began life as parish churches and in some respects retain a parochial flavour although serving primarily as foci of diocesan life. The story of their reordering and of the way in which their spaces are used as settings for the Easter liturgy therefore has relevance for the Church at local level.

The building which in 1927 became the cathedral church of the newly created Diocese of Portsmouth had a long and interesting history. Originally a twelfth-century structure, it was repaired in the seventeenth century after the ravages of the Civil War, significantly enlarged in the 1930s after its designation as a cathedral, and reordered and finally completed in 1991.

By way of contrast, Philadelphia Cathedral is a comparatively new building (1889, rebuilt 1906) in what in American terms is a very old diocese (1784). For complex reasons a cathedral was not established for the Diocese of Pennsylvania until 1992 when, following an abortive new-build project in the 1920s, it was eventually decided to designate as such the Church of the Saviour, at 38th Street and Chestnut.

Before their reordering, both buildings were functional in a basic practical sense, but were severely compromised as spaces for liturgical celebration. Portsmouth was a higgledy-piggledy kind of place which had grown like Topsy over the centuries. It presented a series of poorly related separate rooms, with an unfinished 1930s nave separated from a seventeenth-century classical church by three restricted archways beneath the tower. Philadelphia suffered from the converse problem of a large and wide single undefined space, set out in the 1900s as a typical wealthy neighbourhood church of the period, emphasizing word rather than sacrament and crammed with fixed furniture.

Although Portsmouth had a lot more going for it architecturally than Philadelphia – its twelfth-century original sections, its elegant cupola of 1703, and the handsome work of Nicholson in the 1930s – nevertheless it shared with its trans-Atlantic cousin a lack of liturgical clarity.

Before the wood could be glimpsed, it was necessary to clear some trees. Both buildings had to be as it were 'deconstructed' in order to perceive clearly their bone structure and to recognize their potential as spaces of liturgical celebration. How might they become places where the Easter liturgy could be celebrated with energy and splendour? What had to go? What needed to be enhanced or extended?

Four priorities can be discerned in adapting an existing church building to facilitate the renewed liturgies of the Church, especially those of Easter, and these were evident at both Portsmouth and Philadelphia.

The first requirement was **a place of gathering**; space in which the assembly could gather, be formed, and move forward. Before the Easter liturgy can begin, or be conceived, there needs to be a gathered assembly, a coming together of those who know themselves to be the beloved people of God. An assembly in liturgical terms is very different from a congregation. The latter suggests a collection of individuals, whereas the former is redolent with the Judaeo-Christian narrative of God's covenant people, the *qahal Yahweh*.[3] If the people of God are to realize their true character as an assembly, they need a space in which to gather, and gather not as passive recipients seated in orderly rows facing the front, but as active participants ready to do the work of the people of God, the liturgy.

The nave at Portsmouth, three bays of which had been completed by Nicholson in the 1930s, was extended in 1991 to form a liturgical gathering space of great dignity and beauty.[4] The extended nave forms a square rather than a rectangle, in itself a symbol of active participation – of gathering *around* – and is a light-filled space, thanks to the merciful absence of stained glass. And there is more. A delightful feature of the nave gathering space is the raised ambulatory which surrounds it on four sides, with the nave floor two steps lower. It recalls powerfully the pool of Bethzatha (Bethesda) mentioned in John 5.9, a place likewise surrounded by porticoes. The pool was a place of healing into which the sick stepped down when the waters were troubled by the natural spring bubbling up from below.

The place of gathering and formation is for the assembly likewise a place into which we step down when the 'waters are troubled', that is when our everyday comfort and complacency is disturbed by the Spirit of God as we hear the Scriptures and allow ourselves to be re-formed and reshaped in the pattern of Christ. We step down to immerse ourselves in the waters promised by Jesus which are for us 'a spring of water gushing up to eternal life'.[5]

The task of creating a place of gathering at Philadelphia faced different challenges. The existing nave was large and wide, also forming a basically square shape, but with a floor interrupted by the raised platforms on to which the pews were fixed, and by the grilles of the underfloor heating ducts. The radical development necessary in this case was the clearance from the nave of all existing furniture in order to create a place of active participation rather than passive observance. The pews were removed, the floor levelled, and the mixture of timber and terrazzo floor surfaces replaced with new paving of French limestone throughout. For the first time the spaciousness of the nave and its potential as a gathering place, for both Sunday assembly and the diocese, was realized (sometimes to gasps of amazement).

Not only was the space cleared, but also the visual opulence of the space – stencilled lower walls, coloured clerestory walls, and half-timbered detail above the nave arcade – was drastically toned down. All wall surfaces were repainted a stone colour to produce a room which was a frame for the liturgy, not a counter-attraction at war with it.

The second requirement, of overriding importance in the Easter liturgy, is **a baptismal font**. The gathered assembly is the assembly of the baptized, and its identity as such is a primary focus of any liturgical gathering.[6] Every time it gathers, the assembly recalls who it is at the waters of baptism. To do so we must move beyond the bird baths, salad bowls and covered fonts that masquerade as fitting symbols of our incorporation into Christ. A baptismal font which adequately conveys the concept of God's abundant, overflowing grace needs to be bold, generous and extravagant.

A significant baptismal font is of course central to the Easter liturgy, but water should be evident and accessible in our liturgical spaces at all times. It is not only when baptisms are taking place that a font needs to contain water, but every time the assembly gathers. Here at the font, at every Sunday liturgy, the assembly gathers to recall its vocation, affirm its identity, and renew its life in Christ. For all these reasons, water should be splashing around all over the place. A good font needs to be a pool rather than a puddle.

As a result, both Portsmouth and Philadelphia cathedrals now have baptismal fonts of strength and dignity providing a dominant liturgical focus in the building in which they are set. At Portsmouth the opportunity was seized to place a new font beneath the tower at an axial point of the whole building.

The very nature of the confined space in which it is set is an architectural parable of the narrow gate which leads to life.[7]

The Portsmouth font is of a Greek design typical of the ninth century, and its coffin-like appearance teaches that baptism is in fact a little death, for as Paul reminds us we are baptized into Christ's death that 'we too might walk in newness of life'.[8] The inscription around the rim of the font spells this out:

> When you went down into the water it was like night and you could see nothing. But when you came up again it was like finding yourself in the day. That one moment was your death and your birth: that saving water was both your grave and your mother.   (St Cyril of Jerusalem, *Mystagogical Catecheses* 2.1)

Philadelphia lacked the dramatic architectural possibilities offered by Portsmouth, but placed the font in the wide south aisle of the nave at a point where it is hoped eventually to create a new entrance into the cathedral. This spacious location gives the font prominence and provides ample space for the assembly to gather around it.

The design of the font combines old and new, the original font of the Church of the Saviour moved to this new position and placed alongside a new pool, water cascading continually from old into new, as a symbol of the renewal of the cathedral building and its life. Around the rim of the font another inscription, this time from the Book of Revelation:

> Then the angel showed me the river of the water of life, bright as crystal, flowing from the throne of God and of the Lamb through the middle of the street of the city.[9]

Above the font hangs a corona made of small cast pieces of pewter suspended from the ceiling, each one representing either a person killed on Flight 93 which crashed in Pennsylvania on September 11, 2001, or a baby born in Philadelphia that same day. 'In the midst of life we are in death', yet new life continually bursts forth.

The third requirement is **a progression of spaces**. The assembly of the people of God is a community which throughout the Judaeo-Christian tradition has encountered God on the road. They are a people of journey, God's pilgrim people. An essential feature therefore of church buildings reordered for an awakened sense of liturgical action is a succession of spaces which enable the assembly to experience journey every time it gathers for worship. By this we mean not just a cerebral appreciation of the idea of journey, but an actual journey undertaken by all.

Church buildings with fixed seating and overcrowded interiors present a huge obstacle to our rediscovery of this basic characteristic of our identity and story. Liturgically speaking they shackle us with leg-irons from the past, inhibiting our movement into the future.

Portsmouth enjoyed an embarrassment of riches in terms of spaces within their space, but it was the genius of the 1991 reordering to turn a problem into an advantage. This disjointed and haphazard building was taken and made into a progression of spaces through which the liturgical assembly could make its journey, of particular significance at the Easter liturgy.

At Philadelphia we had to work harder at the journey, for the building didn't give us a head start. Faced with the one big open and level space of the nave, we had to establish different zones of liturgical action by other than architectural means. The construction of the baptismal font created one such liturgical zone. It formed a fixed feature in the midst of its own clearly defined space; a liturgical gathering place for the assembly at the Easter liturgy of course, but also at every Sunday liturgy either for the penitential rite or for the affirmation of faith.

The other two zones of liturgical action – word and sacrament – were established at either end of the nave, defined by liturgical furniture and by seating layout. At the west end, a large ambo reminiscent of a synagogue *bema* was set in the midst of the space, facing east, with chairs placed either side in antiphonal or collegiate style. At the eastern end of the nave the altar table was set in the midst of a large open space with no seating. Ambo and altar stood on the same central axis or liturgical pathway.

Thus in making Eucharist the assembly could journey between three clearly distinguished liturgical zones, each with its distinct focus. In each zone, a different posture of the assembly was appropriate – standing at font and altar table, sitting around the ambo.

Finally, a space for renewed liturgy requires **flexibility**. We are not talking here of the bad old days of dual-purpose buildings in the 1960s, but of liturgical space capable of serving a variety of liturgical needs and of providing several different settings for liturgical action. To take Holy Week as an example, the narrative of events which we are called to enter into moves from market place, to upper room, garden, palace courtyard, place of execution, graveside, upper room again, the lakeside, and the open road. Holy Week takes us through a series of wildly different moods and emotions, from despair to joy. A liturgical space which can set the scene of these events, by changes in appearance, layout and mood, will help us participate more fully and enter more deeply into the mystery.

Flexibility also means that, depending on the season, the direction of liturgical journey can be reversed – for example during Epiphanytide the journey was made from east to west as a sign of our desire to show forth Christ to the world. At other times, in Lent for example, the journey was dispensed with altogether, as we maintained a circular plan of seating around altar table and ambo to mark this period of reflection before embarking on the journey once again as a renewed Easter people.

Now that the stage is set, how were these spaces used for the Easter liturgy, defined for our purpose here as all the liturgies of Holy Week and Easter?

Palm Sunday is the one day of the Church's year when most Christians are used to and comfortable with journey. We get the journey into Jerusalem and make the connection between our Lord's triumphal entry and our own, no matter how disconnected it may seem as we shuffle along, usually half a verse behind the leader, from church hall to worship space.

Not surprisingly, at both Portsmouth and Philadelphia the blessing of palms takes place outside in the cathedral grounds, from which location the assembly processes into the cathedral itself for the liturgy.

The Eucharist of **Maundy Thursday** evening is the most poignant rite of the whole Christian year. It is a time in which the worshipper not only recalls the Last Supper but addresses the question of faithful discipleship, of adherence or betrayal, in one's own life today. When the liturgy of this holy night really speaks to us we are brought face to face with Christ before whom we too, in the accusation of betrayal, are forced to cry out 'Surely not I, Lord?'[10]

The flexibility of the large gathering space in the nave at Philadelphia comes into its own on Maundy Thursday night when a series of trestle tables covered in white cloths are laid end to end down the centre of the nave, and seats arranged on all four sides with the president and assistants at the head. Here is our own 'upper room'. The lighting scheme of the reordered cathedral consists of pendant lights on dimmers which allows the vast space to be transformed into a small intimate room. The assembly is a community of disciples with hard questions to ask of themselves. It is a liturgy for penitence and rededication.

At the beginning of the eucharistic liturgy lots of small night-lights are brought forward and placed along the length of the tables during the singing of the Iona refrain, 'Kindle a flame to lighten the dark'. A form of the customary Scripture readings is used which weaves them together into a continuous narrative, offering a direct commentary on the rite (for this reason the passage from John describing the foot-washing precedes rather than follows the reading from 1 Corinthians).

During the reading from Exodus a pause is made at the appropriate point in the narrative at which small dishes containing samples of the three elements of the Passover meal – roast lamb, bitter herbs and unleavened bread – are laid down the length of the table for the assembly to taste. At the foot-washing, because the community is seated in a large rectangle around the central table, the president and assistants go to members of the assembly in their places.

The cathedral's main altar table is on this night moved to the arcade of arches at the far east end of the cathedral behind the curved stone *presbyterium* containing the bishop's chair, where it serves as the altar of repose. After the eucharistic liturgy at the long nave table, and the stripping of the worship space, the assembly processes to the altar of repose where the customary vigil of prayer is kept until midnight. The whole cathedral is darkened during the Watch, with minimal lighting sufficient only to indicate the route to and from the west door.

At Portsmouth, where a similar liturgical progression is followed, the Chapel of St Thomas at the far east end of the building works extremely well as the place of the altar of repose.

For the liturgy of **Good Friday** the space at Philadelphia is transformed again, this time into a stark and empty space. The lack of fixed furniture in the nave means that this change can be achieved with dramatic effect.

The assembly is seated on two long lines of chairs placed along the north and south colonnades of the nave. The altar table, now bare, remains at the far east end. The bishop and sacred ministers enter to prostrate themselves on the floor of the nave, and move to one side, seated alongside the rest of the assembly. The liturgy is led by the bishop from his seat in the midst of the assembly, and the readings, Passion and prayers are led from the ambo, which remains in place at the west end of the nave facing east. The cross is brought in from the west doors for its proclamation, and placed on the steps leading to the *presbyterium* for the veneration.

The **Great Vigil of Easter Day** (as the American Prayer Book aptly calls it) is of course the litmus test of whether a cathedral space works, and here Portsmouth truly comes into its own. The progression of spaces (in addition to the external space for the lighting of the Easter fire) provided by the cathedral's reordering means that the Easter liturgy can move naturally with the grain of the building through the liturgy.

After the lighting of the fire in the courtyard, the Easter candle is carried into the nave, the place of assembly, for the heart of the Vigil, the recounting in the Hebrew Scriptures of the story of the rescue of God's people from slavery and of their subsequent journeying and longing.

Following the Liturgy of the Word, the rite moves on to the Liturgy of Initiation and the Renewal of Baptismal Vows, for which the font could not be better placed, standing as it does in the centre of the pathway into the place of eucharistic celebration. The assembly then moves eastward into the quire, to gather round the altar table for the Great Thanksgiving.

Thus the progression from one component to the next of the Easter liturgy is facilitated and enhanced at every stage by the progression of spaces in the building. The movement is so natural that it seems the whole place was designed specifically for this purpose. In one way it was, but it took the rethinking and reimagining of the 1991 reordering scheme to draw it all together into a composite whole.

Although Philadelphia is not so fortunate in terms of spatial progression, the building nevertheless, through its spaciousness, openness and flexibility, facilitates beautifully the same journey. The rite takes place before dawn, and the assembly processes from the garden where the Easter fire is blessed, to enter the gathering place at the western end of the nave for the Liturgy of the Word. The *Exsultet* is sung, and the Vigil readings proclaimed, from the ambo in the midst of the nave, the candles around the ambo creating a pool of light in the cavernous darkness. After the *Gloria* is sung and the cathedral filled with light, the assembly moves to the south aisle to gather round the font for the Liturgy of Initiation. Finally the liturgical focus moves to the eastern end of the nave where the whole assembly stands around the altar table to offer the Great Thanksgiving.

Here Philadelphia is at an advantage in that, unlike the quire of Portsmouth, the gathering place for the Great Thanksgiving is empty of chairs, and there is a real and palpable sense of the holy assembly offering the Great Thanksgiving as a prayer of the whole priestly community of God's people. This is symbolized by the invitation of the president (as at every Sunday liturgy) for every member present to place on the floor their service leaflets and to raise their hands in the traditional *orans* posture of prayer to signify their 'full, conscious and active' participation in the priestly prayer.

In summary, no one should run away with the idea that the Easter liturgy as described above is something pertaining only to cathedrals with impressive resources. Philadelphia has for example but one paid member of staff in the music department, and no cathedral choir in the customary sense. The Easter liturgies that take place there, as at Portsmouth, are significant not because they establish a new level of excellence but because they present accessible, attainable goals for any faith community to translate into their own language, situation and way of doing things.

In my own experience I have witnessed the transforming power of the Easter liturgy taking hold of faith communities varying greatly in size, situation and resources. Before the building's restoration, Philadelphia's basement was a gloomy, semi-derelict space, full of 100 years' worth of accumulated junk. On the first Easter of our reconstruction project, however, a dawn Easter Vigil of great beauty and power was celebrated in that most unhelpful and unprepossessing of spaces, because the assembly had glimpsed the glory and were eager to explore.

No matter how unpromising the building or circumstances, it is possible, given the will to do so, to create spaces of gathering and formation, flexible enough to allow the assembly to move and progress, and centred on fonts which do justice to the occasion and help recall the assembly to its true identity as the primary minister of the whole liturgy. Certainly a little ingenuity is required, and sometimes rooms or buildings have to be borrowed and adapted (or pools hired for the weekend!).

Once the assembly has room to move, to progress from one liturgical focus to another, to express itself freely, to make music, to dance, to swing a thurible or two, then we shall have created the kind of space, even if temporary, makeshift, or cobbled together, in which good worship may flourish. In such spaces the assembly comes to realize just who it is; not a congregation of individuals doing their own thing, but the holy priestly people of God fulfilling its sacred task of offering worship in spirit and in truth.[11]

Notes

1 Dirk Lange, *Trauma Recalled: Liturgy, Disruption, and Theology*, Minneapolis, Augsburg Fortress, 2009, pp. 139–40.

2 Matthew 27.32.

3 'In its solemn assemblies Israel could take cognizance of itself as a people called by God, the *qahal Yahweh*.' Catherine Vincie, *Celebrating Divine Mystery*, Collegeville, Liturgical Press, 2009, p. 24.

4 The author is grateful to Nicholas Biddle, Canon Precentor of Portsmouth Cathedral, for his assistance.

5 John 4.14.

6 'The assembly of the baptized comes first, and the fundamental reality of ministry is the ministry of the entire servant church.' Robert W. Hovda, *Strong, Loving and Wise*, Collegeville, Liturgical Press, 1983, p. 3.

7 Matthew 7.13–14.

8 Romans 6.3–40.

9 Revelation 22.1–2.

10 Matthew 26.22.

11 John 4.24.

7

God's patterns: reflections on liturgical shape at Salisbury Cathedral

JEREMY DAVIES

———•◦•———

In his influential little book *The Empty Space*, the celebrated theatre director Peter Brook wrote a critique of what was then the new cathedral in Coventry:

> The new place cries out for a new ceremony, but of course it is the new ceremony that should have come first – it is the ceremony in all its meanings that should have dictated the shape of the place, as it did when all the great mosques and cathedrals and temples were built. Goodwill, sincerity, reverence, belief in culture are not quite enough: the outer form can only take on real authority if the ceremony has equal authority.[1]

Brook goes on in this chapter, entitled 'The holy theatre', to make a claim for the theatre and the artist as the place and the person to recapture the rituals and ceremonies of the holy which were once the domain of the religious and which he, Brook, feels are so no longer. There is more of spiritual gold in Peter Brook's essay to which I shall return, but I start with his provocative suggestion that the ceremony came first and the great cathedrals of the past were then built around its imperatives. There can be few religious buildings of which this observation is more demonstrably the case than at Salisbury. For the creators of Salisbury Cathedral took at least two bites at this particular cherry.

The cathedral at Old Sarum was built at the end of the eleventh century under Bishop Osmund (later to be canonized) as part of the great Norman project to build cathedrals and

119

fortresses across the newly conquered lands. And there the newly formed Diocese of Sarum had its mother church for the next century and a half. Then, whatever the motivation (proximity of the Norman castle and its accompanying rowdiness, perhaps, or the lack of easily accessible water on its windswept hill) the necessary papal permissions were obtained to begin the cathedral anew on a virgin site, at the confluence of several rivers. That in itself was a rarity, for new church buildings are usually extensions or aggrandizements of previously existing shrines. It is because of the reluctance of successive generations to move from their sacred places that most cathedrals show clearly the centuries of architectural development on the same site.

The undoubted inspiration for the move from Old Sarum to New was Richard Poore, who had been dean at the old cathedral and, after a short stint as Bishop of Chichester, returned to Salisbury to succeed his brother as bishop. It was most likely he who put together the regulations relating to the governance of a secular (that is non-monastic) cathedral called the Carta Osmundi (as Poore attempted to elaborate the virtues of his episcopal predecessor whom he tried – without success at this stage – to have canonized). It was Poore also who was responsible for the Consuetudinary, or book of rubrics that gave instructions about the ceremonies of the liturgy and about who does what within the liturgy. Clearly an energetic, forceful man who got things done (he went on as Bishop of Durham to oversee the building of the Chapel of the Nine Altars at the Gothic east end of Durham Cathedral), Richard Poore brought more than a new ground plan to the water meadows of Salisbury. He brought a new mindset, a new vision, a new philosophy. He had been taught in Paris by the finest minds of the Christian West and he was intent on establishing something innovative at Salisbury – hence the new site.

Upon that site within a 38-year building span (1220 to 1258) the prototype of the new architecture in Gothic style was created – to be crowned not long after by the tower and spire. Alongside the new architecture came the new philosophy which was to supersede the old monastic wisdom. Poore brought to Salisbury one of the great scholars of his day (the first person to receive an Oxford Master of Arts), Edmund of Abingdon, who for 11 years was Canon Treasurer of Salisbury before becoming Archbishop of Canterbury (becoming St Edmund shortly after his death in 1246). Clearly the university intended to rival the emerging Oxford never got much beyond the drawing-board (though in the ancient names of Salisbury's streets are vestiges of her academic aspirations), but Salisbury was, nevertheless, intended to be the powerhouse of the modern. And with the architecture, and the learning, and the secular spirituality came a new liturgical pattern. In a sense it was not new at all. The Sarum Use, though it almost certainly owed a great deal to the initiative of Richard Poore, was rooted first of all in the Roman rite of the Western Church. Despite the elaboration and certain unique features of Salisbury's Use and the careful diligence with which liturgical books were copied and conserved at Salisbury (all of which helped to make the Sarum Use the most ubiquitous and widely used liturgical Use in England and Wales and beyond) the Use of Salisbury was recognizably part of the Western rite which had developed from the Use of the papal curia. Allan Doig in his *Liturgy and Architecture* comments, 'the Curial liturgy was progressively simplified, while the Use of Sarum was orderly but highly elaborate', and the architecture was devised in part to accommodate liturgical expedients, for example, 'the podium on which the side-aisle columns sit physically reinforces the notion that the aisles were to accommodate the elaborate processions of the Sarum rite, as were the unusual width and length of the passages of the cloister – the largest, and earliest, surviving in England'.[2]

And furthermore Poore, who had been dean of the old cathedral as well as bishop of the new – knew what a cathedral was for, and that it should be built to express and house the worship of God. He brought to his conception of the new cathedral a sense of how worship should be ordered liturgically. He knew that 'the ceremony must come first', and that 'the ceremony in all its meanings should dictate the shape of the place' for he had had the advantage of having worked out the ceremony that might be appropriate on a smaller scale at another cathedral up the road.

In his wonderfully illustrated book on church architecture David Stancliffe writes:

> However much the great cathedrals such as Salisbury were designed for the processional rites of the core community rather than to contain a large regular congregation the nature of those processional rites had changed. In early centuries the major rites were the Easter liturgy and the rites of initiation and incorporation that derived from it. . . . By the early medieval period processional rites were concerned with marking boundaries between earth and heaven, and patterning the community in the ordered life of the world to come. Rehearsing what God had done for his people in Christ in the dramatic celebrations of the liturgical year and celebrating the lives of the saints in whom that pattern had taken visible root gave an orderly and prescriptive framework to life.[3]

David Stancliffe knows more than most how the nature of the processional rites have changed and indeed how the larger theological and liturgical picture has changed as well since the medieval period, not least in the last 50 years. It is a picture that goes on changing as Christian worshippers and leaders of worship try to discern God's pattern in the maelstrom of competing philosophies, priorities and patterns that is postmodern life. Perhaps the medieval concerns with 'marking boundaries between earth and heaven' and 'the ordered life of the world to come' are not our foremost concerns, and not why processional rites have their value today – which is not to say that ultimate questions about salvation, and the meaning and purpose of human life are not as insistent today as they ever were. We believe that liturgy has the power to express our deepest longings for God in worship and we believe too that liturgy is intimately connected to our pastoral concerns and our apologetic commitments, and so the performance of the liturgy is a key to unlocking many of the doors which appear to bar many people from religious understanding or even religious curiosity.

And liturgy too has the capacity – because it is a pattern of engagement that involves more than words (despite our seeming obsession with words as the final or even the only arbiter of the rational) to open up spaces in our intelligence and imagination and spiritual awareness that would otherwise be closed or segregated. Peter Brook was right – the ceremony must come first – and at Salisbury, as we enter a building whose shape was dictated by the ceremony, we hope that we might learn from the building itself as well as from the community that now inhabits it (as staff, or regular worshippers, or countless visitors) what that ceremony might be with which to articulate the yearnings of the human soul, with which to express our celebration, our prayer and praise, our love and thanksgiving, our shame and pain and our penitence. And most of all a ceremony that knows how to receive as well as give, and which learns to wait in silence for the grace that most amplifies our sense of what it is to be human. Nowhere is that waiting on God more eloquently expressed than in the Easter liturgy.

The Easter liturgy

At the heart of the Christian proclamation is the salvation history brought to a climax and to perfection in the dying and rising of Jesus Christ. And at the heart of our worship lies the liturgical remembering of that salvific event. Christian worship in all its variety, our keeping the weekly remembrance of the resurrection, indeed our daily proclamation of the Lord's death until he comes, springs from our keeping of Easter. Let me quote Peter Brook again, whose strictures about theatrical drama have relevance for our re-enactment of the Easter drama:

> I can take any empty space and call it a bare stage. A man walks across this empty space whilst someone else is watching him, and that is all that is needed for an act of theatre to be engaged.[4]

On Easter morning 'while it is still dark' the crowd assembles, young and old, regular worshipper or curious hanger-on, clergy and laity, together with those about to be plunged into the death and resurrection of the Saviour. We wait in the dark and cold and relative silence outside the church, as though outside a tomb, wondering what will happen. Watching to see if someone will indeed enter the empty space and an act of drama will be engaged in. This is how, at Salisbury Cathedral, we begin the most important liturgy of the Christian calendar – with nothing except an empty space. It is true a bonfire has been built; we carry in our hands the order of service which in the dark we cannot read, and the ministers of the rite are already dressed for a celebration. But are they all dressed up with nowhere to go? The bishop greets us, we hear the old story of how once upon a time when Israel was a slave in Egypt, God entered the empty space, led his people through the sea to safety and a promised land. And, at this point by way of illustration, the great fire is lit as we hear of the fiery pillar which led the Hebrews out of bondage. Actually, though the fire at Salisbury is immense, the point of the fire is simply to provide the flame with which the Easter candle is lit. First the candle is pierced with the five marks of Christ's passion, to remind us that there is no resurrection from the dead without passing through the valley of death, no passing through the waters of destruction before drowning in their depths. An act of drama has been engaged in; the space is empty no more. It throngs with people who have come to life in the firelight. They are ready for a journey – like the Hebrews of old, they are coated, and hatted, and clutch their bags. But are they properly equipped? They are given two things at the start of their journey: a light flickering in the cold dark, and a snatch of song as the deacon raising the lit candle proclaims the light of Christ, and the people, repeating the chant, respond: Thanks be to God. With this meagre equipment – the light of Christ and a snatch of chant with which to proclaim that this is so – the people of God begin their procession, their journey.

The procession is not just a liturgical pattern but a life's pilgrimage, renewed under God. We move into the church, still dark and tomb-like, and little by little as the sun's rays peep over the eastern horizon, the candlelight drawn from the Paschal presence is passed from person to person and illuminates the building in a sacramental re-enactment of the life of the Church.

Into this assembly and supported by this assembly come those to be baptized and confirmed, rather as those who heard the apostle Peter on an Easter morning in the early Church. There is an illuminating essay by the New Testament scholar the late F. L. Cross, who evocatively suggested that the first epistle of Peter might indeed be an eponymous work and that what we have here is less a letter and more a liturgical text – the bishop's text indeed as he exhorts and encourages and then baptizes those early Christians, probably slaves, into the royal priesthood, the holy nation of the people elected by God.[5] Whether or not Cross is right, the presence of the bishop baptizing and confirming new Christians as the sun rises on Easter Day powerfully enacts the first epistle of Peter.

The neophytes remain at the font at the cathedral's west end while the assembly continues to light the church with its lamps and fill it, tomb that it once was, with the fragrant embalming spices which have now become the perfume of a new Jerusalem. Then at the spire crossing at the heart of the church, where just a few days before, the shroud of the crucified was symbolically laid, the *Exsultet* or Song of Praise is sung to celebrate the candle which symbolizes the risen Christ. Then the Easter proclamation is made, and the congregation responds with the ringing of bells and sounding of gongs and cymbals, and loud peals on the organ. A moment of spontaneous and exuberant disorder that would gladden the heart of any charismatic worshipper! After the singing of the Gloria and the reading of a passage from the epistle to the Romans, the procession returns to the font, where those to be baptized still wait to be incorporated into the company of the baptized. At the font, the Gospel is read, the new water is blessed, the confession of faith is made and the catechumens, having turned to Christ and been marked by his Passion, affirm that this is indeed their faith, and with much pouring of water new Christians are made. They discover in a way not to be forgotten that God has called them by name and made them his own.

But this is no time to rest. We should ideally clothe the newly baptized in white robes and give each of them a glass of milk (as 1 Peter suggests that those first Christians might have done). Instead we give them a candle for the onward journey, and they and the whole assembly move again through the building to the point where those to be confirmed have hands laid on them, and are anointed with the precious oil of chrism, newly blessed on the previous Thursday, to reinforce the sense of their entry into the royal priesthood and to strengthen them for their witness to the risen Christ.

Then again the assembly moves on towards the high altar, where the banquet has been prepared. The body broken and the blood outpoured, which we solemnly commemorated just two days before, now become the source of nourishment and grace and the means by which the body (which is the Church) is made whole – made whole indeed so that the body may be broken again and again in compassionate service and evangelical witness outside the shrine. For the procession and pilgrimage which the Easter liturgy embodies only begins here: it carries on into the street and into the world for which Christ died and rose again.

Actually we have a moment's deviation from our mission to party, in response to Jesus' command to his disciples to come and have breakfast. The procession moves out of the church singing *Surrexit Dominus Vere* and circles the cloister to the sound of champagne corks popping before a lavish, convivial breakfast is enjoyed, reminding us that despite the arduousness of the journey we are an Easter people and Alleluia is our song.

I have taken some time to describe the Easter liturgy at Salisbury Cathedral because that liturgy is so central to our understanding of our faith, our experience of it and our practical outworking of it. It has often been said: if you want to know what Anglicans believe, attend and enter into their worship. I would go further. If you want to grasp what Christians believe, enter into the liturgical pattern of their Easter celebrations. That pattern of celebration is worth more than a hundred sermons or tutorials in the faith, not least because words are for a moment silenced and out of the silence and the cold and the darkness, 'the empty space', God re-creates his world and his people and establishes again his redemptive purpose.

All other liturgies in Salisbury Cathedral take their bearings from this one. None of the others is quite as homespun or quite as chaotic, as order by degrees emerges out of the disorder of the motley assembly, but they all convey the sense of the holy common people of God on the move – even when most of the people of God are firmly seated in their pews! The procession helps us all to enter into the journey imaginatively, helped of course by the movement, the colour, the music, the lights and smells, the words too and perhaps most of all the silence, which corresponds to the much needed stopping places on a physical pilgrimage.

Pastoral offices: rites of initiation

Given the picture thus painted of the Easter liturgy, it will be no surprise that the rites which most accord with the Easter drama are the rites of initiation which take place regularly in the cathedral. Again, the emphasis is on pilgrimage and the sense that the Christian experience is not a one-off or even a once-for-all experience, even though we may have had some form of disclosure experience that has turned our lives around. It is the sense of transformation and renewal that should distinguish the liturgy of the Church. So often it is reported that church services are dull and boring. Such services may not entertain us but if, as I am suggesting, they are found to be life-transforming and renewing we will expect them to be demanding and to raise questions about our life choices – but dull and boring? There is certainly a requirement that priests and other worship leaders will use some imagination in their planning, preparation and presentation of the liturgy so that worship doesn't fall into the rut of the routine. And this will inevitably involve some grasp of liturgical principles and a realistic understanding of how these principles can be enacted with the often limited resources – architectural space, music, personnel – that are available. But worship does not have to be grand to be transformative. Even in the spacious opportunities of cathedrals and large churches the most effective worship is often the most simple – and, as the foregoing reflection on the Easter liturgy intimated, we come to God with our poverty, our disorder and our empty spaces, and it is God himself who gives us the simple and seemingly meagre resources with which to weave our praise.

At diocesan rites of initiation something of that Easter pattern is recalled. The lights are again turned off and we are plunged into darkness (the symbolism is lost of course when these rites take place on a blazing summer evening!). Out of the darkness comes a reading of the Genesis account of the making of the light. The Paschal candle is again lit to the accompaniment of the Taizé chant *Veni Sancte Spiritus* (rehearsed with the congregation before the service starts). The involvement of a single solo voice, the response of the congregation and the reading of a passage of Scripture while the chant is being sung gathers the whole assembly together and brings us to a place of prayer and palpable silence – as the oft-repeated Taizé chants are intended to do. From our waiting in silence we move to praise – the lights come on and we are on more familiar territory with a well known hymn. During this the procession with the bishops (typically all three bishops will take part in these diocesan occasions) enters. All the candidates gather, with their sponsors and those who have prepared them, at the west end of the building where they are presented to, and greeted by, the bishops. The presiding bishop signs with the cross those who are to be baptized – at these services the newly baptized are adults or young people able to answer for themselves. Often the various stages of the liturgy are accompanied by a short word of encouragement from one of the bishops, but despite the richness of the *Common Worship* texts for the initiation rites and our tendency to think that liturgy is not valid if not spoken, the main emphasis of our Salisbury liturgies is on the sense of movement and pilgrimage, a sense that we move together as God's people – bishops and laity, young and old, new to the faith or well established or curious family friend, and a sense, as with the Easter liturgy, that it is the simple but eloquent sacramental acts and symbols that impart grace and speak to us as words alone never can.

At the font we hear Scripture read, a short homily is offered, and the candidates for baptism are well and truly deluged in water even though not immersed. Our splendid new font at Salisbury is beautiful, large and unignorable. It stands at the converging points of the main concourse so that visitor and worshipper alike are drawn, fascinated, to it. It reminds us all, not just at these baptismal offices, of the Christian life into which by our baptism we have been drawn. The water in the font is always flowing – not just an unrefreshed stagnant puddle which it so often becomes in our churches – and as visitors pass it or a church procession enters, we dip our hands and make the sign which at our own baptism was etched on our foreheads. The newly baptized – looking half drowned – will remember from the experience that the drowning followed by the drying has something deeper to imply about death and resurrection, and about grace transforming human fallibility. There is a lot of hilarious sprinkling of the people to make the point. Maybe the hilarity runs the risk of undermining the seriousness of what has been undertaken, but I have to remind myself that this is a pilgrimage, and every journey however determined needs its lighter moments.

And so, thus renewed and with the Paschal candle again leading us, we move as a very disorderly but happy crowd to our next gathering point at the heart of the cathedral at the spire crossing. There after a reading from the Gospel the three bishops together (but separately!) lay hands on the heads and anoint with the oil of chrism the candidates for confirmation.

If water is the sign of baptism, oil is the sacramental sign that confirms our Christian allegiance and our membership of the royal priesthood. At long last the Church of England has grasped the fact that baptism is the primary rite of initiation (not confirmation) and that our spiritual journey continues from that point with staging-posts – admission to communion, confirmation, and other significant thresholds (marriage, ordination, birth of children, death itself) – marking that onward pilgrimage towards, and in the company of, the divine. The liturgical procession, imaginatively realized, is a dramatic way of reinforcing that sense of spiritual pilgrimage. Not all baptisms will be so public, so well attended or so theatrical, but the underlying principles still need to be enacted and the sense of performance and movement conveyed. The conclusion of the rite (which may or may not include a celebration of Holy Communion) involves the giving of lighted candles to those just baptized and confirmed, as the rest of the assembly bids them 'Shine as a light in the world to the glory of God the Father'. Bearing their lighted candles they then move to the cathedral's west end to applause. Quite rightly they are made to feel the centre of attention; they are the rite's celebrities. But the candle they carry is a sign of who the real celebrity is and it also reminds them that the pilgrimage does not end when the procession ends. Indeed this is only just the beginning.

Going out and coming in are important thresholds in any liturgy which are given scant recognition in our liturgical texts. Perhaps this is understandable since doors are merely passports to more interesting parts of our life. I am interested that Jesus describes himself as the door, though this is one of the famous Johannine 'I am' sayings that receives least attention. But if we expect our liturgical experience to be a transformative experience then our expectations will be high as we enter and our commitment and enthusiasm high as we leave. Certainly other pastoral offices – such as marriages and funerals – have a lot to teach us about coming in and going out, for they point, as all sacraments do, beyond the sacramental moment to some universal truth about what it is to be human. Brides and grooms

enter church separately, traditionally supported respectively by
the bride's father and the best man. They leave church different
people, legally and spiritually, as a result of the half-hour or so
in church. And their procession out, leading the congregation,
is a threshold moment as they face the world together. Equally
the coming in and going out of a coffin at a funeral is a poignant moment. Receiving a coffin and sprinkling it with holy
water as a reminder of the deceased's baptism, and censing
and sprinkling it at the commendation are appropriate ways
of honouring a dead person as a child of God. But they are
also sacramental moments that take us beyond the local and
the particular. We are all mortal, we shall all die. The sprinkling
and the censing that mark this person's incoming and outgoing
are reminders that the bell tolling tolls for us too, and that
the God who calls us in baptism is the same God who holds
us through death and beyond it with the promise (which we
repeat at a Salisbury funeral commendation though it is taken
in fact from the *Common Worship* confirmation rite) that God
has called us by name and made us his own.

Advent, Christmas and Epiphany

No consideration of Salisbury processions would be complete
without some reference to the spectacular and dramatic series
of processions that mark Advent, Christmas and Epiphany
when, along with the celebrations of Holy Week, the cathedral
feels that it is entering into the liturgical heritage of our
medieval forebears while at the same time recognizing how that
tradition has changed imaginatively in order to speak anew to
the contemporary world of the things of God.

In 2010 Salisbury Cathedral experimented for the first time
with three Advent processions on three consecutive evenings,
so great had been the pressure of demand. A whole range
of motives draws people in these numbers year after year to
Salisbury. The beauty of the building, of course, but more the
drama, the sense of mystery, the beauty of the music and the
compelling narrative as the salvation history is told from Old

Testament to New. No sermon is required as a packed cathedral waits in the darkness for a single candle to be lit, from which some two thousand other candles are gradually lit. And the procession is on this occasion a kind of arabesque of movement in music and light as choir and clergy perform an elaborate counterpoint to the antiphonal reading of Scripture from different ends of the cathedral as Old Testament prophecy finds its answer in New Testament fulfilment.

Perhaps more obviously coherent is the Christmas procession (two at the time of writing) where again we move from west to east in procession, but with more lights available from the start allowing earlier congregational participation than the Advent procession can perforce allow. This time the Christmas crib at the spire crossing is the focal point of the procession. Three processions move simultaneously towards the crib – the two choir processions flanking the central procession as the clergy accompany the Word of God, which is read by lay members of the cathedral staff and congregation at different points in the building. At the crib we are all brought to our knees in adoration while the choir sings Rossetti's famous poem 'In the bleak mid-winter'. The crib is censed and blessed by the bishop, but then the procession moves us on (as our Christmas celebrations all too often do not) from the crib. The procession takes us eastwards into the quire as we hear the story of the magi, and then to the high altar where John's reflection on the Word made flesh is proclaimed (as a foretaste of its being sung into the black night sky at the processional end of the midnight mass). We return to the crib in the final hymn to genuflect there before we move on and out, with the message of the Word made flesh delivered to us for our further reflection and subsequent proclamation. In the prologue to this Christmas procession there is a reflection on the theological imperative that undergirds it:

> The Christmas Procession concentrates on two movements of love. First of all, God comes close to us – and we are reminded how this divine intervention in our lives takes place, as we hear the story which still has the power to stop us in our tracks, make

us catch our breath and turn our hearts. That story located in first century Palestine still draws us because its message remains true: God is with us. He has entered our life with his love, and can never extricate himself from it. And the crib at the centre of this Procession reminds us that this is true.

The other movement that is made in this service is the movement we make towards God. There are too many people in the cathedral for us all, physically, to make the procession to the crib. Others – our representatives – will make that journey, not just for us, but with us. Each of us has the opportunity to move in imagination, to make a spiritual journey, even though we barely leave our seats. The movement towards God requires an openness to his presence – no more. There will be many things in this service to help our God-ward progress – readings from the scriptures, candlelight, beautiful music, the sense of wonder in a crowded ancient building – but the point of all these ceremonies of great beauty is much simpler and starker: God is closer to us than the candles we hold in our hands, and he longs to burn within our hearts.

The Epiphany procession is celebrated sometime in the Epiphany season to remind us precisely of that fact (that Epiphany is a season as well as a feast) and to this end we keep our crib as a focus of devotion throughout the 40 days of Christmas until 2 February. Believing this season to be a revelation of God's glory to the whole world and as a call to renewed discipleship, our Epiphany procession begins at the high altar, where the bishop blesses incense and we recall the three miracles that characterize the Epiphany celebration – the story of the magi, the miracle at Cana and the baptism of Jesus. Those three epiphanies provide the substance of the biblical narrative. But as with all liturgical expression we endeavour to make the revelation of God a contemporary event with all its challenge and inspiration. So, for example, the gifts of the magi recall our own pattern of prayer and devotion, and our ministries of care and compassion to others. The baptism of Jesus recalls us to our own discipleship within the community of the baptized and our prayers are led by those who have recently been baptized. And the wedding at Cana (though it offers huge scope for wider hermeneutic reflection) allows us to focus on and give thanks for human companionship and our prayers are led by two who have in the past year solemnized their relationship. As our Epiphany procession moves, unusually, from east to west, our Christian allegiance is reaffirmed in words of commitment from the Methodist Covenant service. Thus empowered the great west doors of the cathedral are flung wide as the people end the procession, only to begin their pilgrimage in the dark night so that they too may be lights to enlighten the nations. And God's pattern into which we have entered liturgically becomes a road map of the spirit as we seek to sing the Lord's song in a strange land.

Notes

1 Peter Brook, *The Empty Space*, London, Penguin Modern Classics, 2008, p. 51.

2 Allan Doig, *Liturgy and Architecture: From the Early Church to the Middle Ages*, Aldershot, Ashgate, 2008, p. 190.

3 David Stancliffe, *The Lion Companion to Church Architecture*, Oxford, Lion, 2008, p. 129.

4 Brook, *The Empty Space*, ch. 1, 'The Deadly Theatre', p. 11.

5 F. L. Cross, *1 Peter: A Paschal Liturgy*, London, Mowbray, 1954.

Part 3

COMMON WORSHIP: TOMORROW'S LITURGY

8

Forming the practitioners

PETER MOGER

—•◆•—

A new way of doing liturgy

The advent of *Common Worship* in 2000 heralded a new way of doing liturgy in the Church of England. Although some of the contents of the *Common Worship* family of volumes were revised versions of extant material, *Common Worship* is far from simply the result of a process of liturgical revision. The richest provision for worship the Church has known since the Reformation, *Common Worship* has sought to resource and enable a wide range of liturgical practice within what has become known as a 'mixed-economy Church'. This is made clear in the Preface to the main volume, which states, 'The services provided here are rich and varied. This reflects the multiplicity of contexts in which worship is offered today.'[1] Ten years on, there is an ever greater liturgical diversity than in 2000, and as 'Fresh Expressions' of church push at the boundaries of what is allowably Anglican, some are asking whether *Common Worship* provides enough variety while others are lamenting the fast disappearing notion of a common prayer for the Church of England.

Not only does *Common Worship* encompass a wider range of liturgical material than before, its publication also reflects a desire to bring together 'treasures old and new' – the traditional and the contemporary. Whereas the *Alternative Service Book 1980* had been a conscious alternative to the Book of Common Prayer, *Common Worship* sought to include a significant quantity of traditional language material, much from the BCP itself, alongside contemporary texts. As such, *Common Worship* stands more as a product of a postmodern age, in stark contrast to its predecessors.

Common Worship also ushered in a new era of liturgical publishing in the Church of England. It is significant that its title is not *The Book* (or even *books*) of *Common Worship*, for although the contents of *Common Worship* may be found in a family of volumes, equally important is the fact that all the material is available in electronic form. The accessibility of the texts both on the Church of England website (<www.churchofengland.org/prayer-worship/worship/liturgical-texts.aspx>) and as part of the *Visual Liturgy* software produced by Church House Publishing has meant that planners and leaders of worship have been able to select, cut and paste texts in the course of creating liturgy which, while following a common structure and containing some common elements, is specific to the local context of worship and mission.

New needs for training and formation

Common Worship marks an enormous shift – from a 'book' culture to a 'download, cut and paste' culture. Hence it is no longer possible to lead a service simply by opening a service book at a particular page and reading the content until reaching the end, as was true with the BCP and (to a slightly lesser extent) the *ASB*. This has significant implications for liturgical training. No longer is it sufficient for training to consist of a course of liturgical history together with the imparting of a bank of skills in delivering a limited range of fixed services. More than ever before, there is a need for the thorough liturgical formation of those training for public ministry.

Would-be worship leaders (lay and ordained) are in need of a solid grounding in the liturgical principles of structure and flow, based on an understanding of worship as a transformative process. There is greater need for a clear understanding of the times and seasons of the Christian year, and of the interplay of Scripture, liturgy and theology. And the move away from theme-based lectionaries to a greater proportion of *lectio continua* throughout the year necessitates a more systematic approach to the role of the Bible in worship. Ministers need to be equipped to make intelligent choices, to develop the practice of thinking liturgically and, in a 'mixed-economy' Church, to engage in practical learning across a range of contexts and traditions.

All this throws up an immense challenge for the liturgical formation of the current and future generations of ordained and licensed ministers – to say nothing of those already in ministry who were brought up on older, more fixed, models of liturgical practice. The challenge stretches across both periods of Initial Ministerial Education (IME): 1–3 (the years of training at college, or on a course or scheme) and 4–7 (the years immediately following ordination or licensing), and beyond into the years of Continuing Ministerial Education (CME) and Development.

Transforming worship

As the *Common Worship* enterprise ran its course, it became increasingly clear to the Liturgical Commission that, once the task of drafting texts was complete, its major challenge would be one of training and formation: equipping those responsible for the planning and leadership of worship within the Church of England to make best use of the material.

This process began initially through the Commission's Formation Group in the 2001–2005 quinquennium. Working under the constraint of trying to set a formation agenda at the same time as drafting new liturgical texts, the group sponsored a number of training events. Its major achievement, though, was to secure funding for the post of National Worship Development Officer (NWDO) from 2005, following many years of lobbying on the part of Commission members and the then chairman, Bishop David Stancliffe. The placing of a dedicated liturgical formation post within the National Church Institutions (NCIs) at Church House, Westminster, enabled some joined-up thinking to take place between the Liturgical Commission and the various Divisions of the NCIs, keeping worship on the agenda and helping stress in particular the links which exist between well-executed worship and fruitful mission.

In planning for the 2006–2010 quinquennium, it became clear that, as the generation of texts for worship was drawing to an end – with the publication of *Ordination Services* (2005), *Christian Initiation* (2006), *Times and Seasons* (2006) and *Festivals* (2008) – it would be possible for the Commission to centre its efforts on formation. This was reflected both in the membership of the 2006–2010 Commission and, following the appointment of the NWDO, the launch of the *Transforming Worship* initiative.

Transforming Worship was presented to the General Synod of the Church of England at York in July 2007 with a Report *Transforming Worship: Living the New Creation* (GS 1651).[2] This set out some helpful criteria for liturgical formation before going on to enumerate particular areas of challenge for the Church, among which were included recommendations that

- each diocese should have a Diocesan Liturgical Committee (DLC) or equivalent group
- diocesan CME officers draw up a comprehensive programme of liturgical training for IME 4–7
- DLCs pay special attention to supporting mutual learning and critical thinking among parishes using new media in worship
- congregations attend to the ways in which they can provide for the inclusion of children fully in their worship
- bishops reflect together on the ways in which they try to promote good liturgy within their dioceses
- the House of Bishops CME Committee develop a programme of liturgical training
- an agreed set of core practical competencies and skills for IME 1–3 be drawn up to support the learning outcomes in the Ministry Division document *Shaping the Future*
- the National Society work with the Liturgical Commission, dioceses, and Regional Training Partnerships (RTPs), to train and resource ministers in preparing and leading school worship.

The years immediately following the publication of the Report have seen encouraging progress in a number of these areas. Particularly exciting has been the joint Liturgical Commission/ National Society/Royal School of Church Music (RSCM) *Resourcing School Worship* project, which is on course to deliver an online liturgy and song resource for school worship. A group from the Commission has drawn up a set of core practical competencies and skills in worship for IME 1–3, and work has continued through Praxis to devise a 'syllabus' for liturgical formation in IME 4–7. The General Synod asked in 2008 for additional Eucharistic Prayers for occasions when significant numbers of children are present, opening the way for further work in the field of children's and multi-generational worship. Liturgical CME for bishops has also found a place on the regular list of episcopal training opportunities.

In the report, the Commission also set out its desire to work collaboratively with those bodies and organizations already active in the field of liturgical formation. Partnership became increasingly important in the years which followed, with the Commission joining in projects and training ventures with Praxis, the Alcuin Club, the Group for the Renewal of Worship (GROW), RSCM, Music and Worship Foundation, the Prayer Book Society, the Church of England Evangelical Council, and the Hospital Chaplaincies Council as well as the dioceses and the Education, Mission and Public Affairs, Ministry and Communications Divisions within the NCIs.

The Commission's own 'roadshows' have also formed an important part of the *Transforming Worship* initiative. Following the pattern of a series of training days on the *Common Worship* ordinal in 2006, subjects covered have included Liturgical Presidency, Liturgy and Church Buildings and All-Age Worship. In the last of these, the Commission owes a great debt to the authors (and in particular to the editor, Gill Ambrose) of *Together for a Season*, a three-volume collection of liturgical resources for all-age worship which derive from the *Times and Seasons* and *Festivals* volumes of *Common Worship*.[3]

In 2008, the Liturgical Commission published *Worship Changes Lives*,[4] a non-technical illustrated 48-page book about liturgy which, together with supporting study materials, has been promoted and used as a resource by a number of dioceses. The following year, Peter Moger (with Tim Lomax) published *Crafting Common Worship*.[5] This set out some of the principles underpinning *Common Worship*, and addressed the question of what it means for material to be authorized or commended, before going on to give practical examples of how *Common Worship* material might be used to achieve flexibility and local variety within the prescribed frameworks.

Four years after the appointment of the NWDO, though, the impact of an Archbishops' Council spending review began to bite. In October 2009, following the move of Colin Podmore to increased responsibilities with the Dioceses Commission, the post of NWDO was combined with that of Secretary of the Liturgical Commission. Then, on the departure of Peter Moger in the summer of 2010, this combined post was further reduced to a half-time appointment. It is regrettable that, following the Herculean efforts of those on the Commission prior to 2005 to secure a national formation post, the Church of England has seen fit to reduce national senior staff support for worship (its core activity) to 0.5 of a post.

This reduction of national resourcing has put the ball firmly in the court of the dioceses and the RTPs, all of which struggle to balance training priorities with ever diminishing funds.

Some challenges for the future

Perhaps the greatest challenge we face is the provision of adequate Initial Ministerial Education in the field of liturgy. Liturgical formation at both IME 1–3 and IME 4–7 is currently patchy, to say the least. Fewer than half of the residential theological colleges now employ a specialist tutor of liturgy and worship. Those who do, experience the benefit of having a staff member who not only teaches the subject but is also a core member of the college's worshipping community, thus embodying the link between liturgical teaching and practical experience of worship. For the growing proportion of those who train for ministry on non-residential courses and schemes, the likelihood of their receiving any sustained input on the principles and practice of liturgy is not great. Here, time constraints are a major problem, with tutors forced to condense teaching into an impossibly tight time-frame.

The result of this situation – which is not new but which has been steadily worsening over the past two decades – is that fewer newly ordained or licensed ministers have a clear understanding of liturgical principles or an awareness of what resources exist. Many of those in training or new to public ministry are simply unaware of the contents and scope of *Common Worship*, and even still less how to use it.

'Fresh Expressions of church' offer a distinctive challenge to the liturgical status quo. Often 'on the edges' of traditional parish structures, these initiatives find themselves in situations in which the perceived needs of worshippers might be seen to be at variance with the official liturgical provision. Maintaining a balance between effective mission on one hand and faithfulness to the inherited Anglican understanding of worship on the other is proving challenging in some places. An Appendix to the Dioceses, Pastoral and Mission Measure 2007[6] sets out the essential 'bottom line' but it is clear that this issue will continue to raise its head well into the future. In addition, given the high degree of liturgical flexibility in many Fresh Expressions, it would seem important that pioneer ministers and others involved in their leadership should be exceptionally well grounded in good liturgical principles, if the worship that emerges is to be genuinely both fresh and Anglican.

The *Transforming Worship* report recommended that each diocese should have a liturgical group (or equivalent). Following the withdrawal of central church support for liturgy and worship, the need for this has never been greater: it is clear that dioceses and regions are going to have to bear the brunt of formation work if there is to be any progress. Some dioceses have already grasped the need to resource and deliver training within the diocese, often working closely with the training team and those responsible for IME 4–7. Building on the RTP model, collaboration among neighbouring dioceses is an obvious way forward, sharing gifts and expertise to best effect.

Some of the greatest successes, though, in terms of active and fruitful liturgical formation work, have been seen in those few dioceses which have invested in dedicated (stipendiary) worship officers. The evidence is that, even where such an officer is effectively part-time, the DLC (or equivalent group) is better able to support the delivery of quality training. Perhaps most significant here has been the work done by Helen Bent, the Bishop's Adviser for Music and Worship in the Diocese of Sheffield. Under her leadership, the diocese has been able to resource a programme of training in worship, and to pioneer *Worship 4 Today*,[7] a course for lay worship leaders from a wide range of backgrounds and traditions, which is already having an impact beyond the boundaries of the diocese. Looking to the future, if more dioceses were prepared to invest in worship officers, the outlook for liturgical formation might look rather less bleak than it does at present.

Notes

1 *Common Worship: Services and Prayers for the Church of England*, London, Church House Publishing, 2000.

2 *Transforming Worship: Living the New Creation*, A Report by the Liturgical Commission, GS 1651, London, Church House Publishing, 2007 – also at <www.transformingworship.org>.

3 Gill Ambrose (ed.), *Together for a Season: All-age Seasonal Resources*, 3 vols, London, Church House Publishing, 2006–9.

4 Paul Bradshaw and Peter Moger (eds), *Worship Changes Lives: How it Works, Why it Matters*, London, Church House Publishing, 2008.

5 Peter Moger (with case studies by Tim Lomax), *Crafting Common Worship: A Practical Guide to What's Possible*, London, Church House Publishing, 2009.

6 *The Ordering of Worship in Fresh Expressions of Church under Bishops' Mission Orders*, quoted in Moger, *Crafting Common Worship*, pp. 158–61.

7 <http://sheffield.anglican.org/index.php/church-in-action/ministry-mission-training-and-development/music-and-worship/worship-4-today/144-worship-4-today>.

9

Liturgical future

GILLY MYERS

———————◆◆◆———————

Introduction

More than the night watch . . .

> My soul waits for the Lord,
> more than the night watch for the morning,
> more than the night watch for the morning.[1]

A few years ago my family visited Disneyland. We had a three-day pass, and made the most of the time to explore the self-styled Happiest Place on Earth. Everything about the park marketed the dream. The crowd was almost unwittingly swept up in the wonder of this belief, the place where all is perfect and everything turns out all right in the end. The fairytales and stories of our youth came to life before us, and all were drawn deeply into them, with choreographed excitement and heightened awareness, ready to be filled with comfort and bold hope.

The dream was pervasive – whether it was the warm and reassuring greeting by an over-sized Disney cartoon character, the multi-coloured, music-filled parades, the jovial, helpful characters at the food outlets or the amazing extended firework display at the close of the day – an effervescence of glistening colours dancing, fizzing and exploding evocatively in time to the well-known ebb and flow of the movie tunes. How hard it was to leave such a place.

Yet everyone did leave, of course, and we reflected on how it is that people so rarely depart from an act of Christian worship with such a longing to get more of what they have just experienced. The Church does not have the marketing resources of Disney Enterprises but, in contrast to the frothy wonder and fleeting sparkles, our hope has real substance, and we gather with the possibility of being drawn deeper into the presence of the living God!

Do we come to worship with anticipation? Do we expect something to happen when we worship? Do those who prepare and lead the worship imagine the possibility of God's rushing wind to knock us off our feet? If there is to be any future for liturgy and worship in the Church, then we must never cease to be expectant, to wait for the Lord – just as the night watch of the psalmist waits in eager longing for the first sign of sunrise, knowing that it will surely come.

Expectation needs to be nurtured – to be imagined and held as a real possibility. We need to help one another to be expectant, and to be imaginative in what we expect. Imaginative in the scene-setting, too, preparing an environment like a carefully stacked pile of kindling wood, ready to be ignited by a spark into a flaming fire; imaginative to the possibilities of an engaging encounter with God as we worship, opening ourselves to the opportunity, allowing space for the Spirit of God to sweep through the gathered community and set the worship alight.

In the Scriptures we snatch an occasional glimpse of heaven, and gain an insight into how awe-inspiring worship can be where there is no distraction and all have a common purpose, gathered around, and in the midst of the dazzling presence of God. This is where we can begin, as we look to the liturgical future.

Unlike the Disney experience, worship is not for our sakes, it is for God's sake. And by God's grace, as we worship, we might be taken deeper into heaven, deeper into the knowledge of the Godhead. As we worship, we find hope, comfort, faith, challenge, vision and vocation. We are changed, transformed, renewed and equipped for mission and service in the kingdom of heaven.

This is the essence of worship, and we hold on to this, as we explore some of the detailed considerations of Church of England liturgy in the years to come.

Looking ahead

If I were able to use only one word to describe the liturgical future of the Church of England, it would be 'diverse'. Diversity is not new, of course. Hard-and-fast uniformity probably began to hit the dust almost as soon as it was introduced. During the past couple of centuries, the combination of the adoption of various alternative or additional liturgical practices, and the expanding number of options characteristic of recent liturgical revision, has led us on to radically new terrain. What we find, now, is that a huge and rich diversity has been embraced within the authorized provision of the Church of England.

This opens up tremendous opportunities for imagination and creativity. Some have been anxious at the loss of uniformity, but I rejoice in the variety, and in the opportunities that it brings. It gives people in very different contexts the authorization to worship in very different ways – each appropriate for them, using words, sounds, symbols, and so on, that resonate within the culture in which they are set. Each is able to develop their worship with imagination and creativity.

We know that, as human beings, we are not all the same, and we do not all respond in the same way to a single worshipping environment or experience. Maybe we can understand this in terms of soil types. What a difference the soil can make to the flourishing of a plant: a cactus will thrive in a desert, whereas bulrushes do best in damp, marshy conditions. Preparing the ground for worship can make such a difference, too – and the diversity of our authorized resources opens up the possibilities for many contexts, ministers in each being able to lay the ground, or prepare the soil for an appropriate act of worship that will enable that transportation into the heavenly realms.

It is also important to remember that the introduction of *Common Worship* has been consistently accompanied by reminders that worship is more than the texts and Bible readings – more than the words that are said or sung in a service. The components of this fertile soil include many other factors: the people; place and time of day; furniture and layout of the space; lighting and colour; music, sounds and silence; delivery and interpretation of Scripture; symbol, images and art; other sensory experience, such as aroma and temperature; pacing and rhythm of the service; movement; drama, action and involvement; leadership.

In each act of worship, the mix of the soil is determined by the permutation of these components. The challenge is to get the balance right.

Training for diversity

Tools of the trade

At one point I worked in a cathedral that had its own stone yard and a number of full-time stonemasons. The cathedral was part of a national scheme which nurtures young people with the skills and knowledge to continue this centuries-old traditional craft. Medieval cathedrals are not the only historic buildings to need almost constant attention to the stone-work, and there is a need for these skills to be passed on to each generation. This scheme provided for young men and women to spend time as apprentices in the stone yard, to gain experience alongside experienced practitioners, to acquire the necessary skills and to learn how to use their many tools, implements and materials.

The importance of training and learning applies as much to those who plan and lead worship in our churches, as to those who work in stone. Considering the amount of choice before us, and the complex art of crafting an act of worship when we have such freedom, the necessity for comprehensive liturgical training is greater now than ever before.

Common Worship and the Book of Common Prayer comprise the basic tool-box of the worship leader. In order to craft a service to the very best of our ability, ministers and worship leaders need to know:

- the contents of the tool-box
- the basic purpose of each tool – what it is for
- the potential of each tool – what it can do
- how to use the tool
- the nature of the raw material with which they are working.

What's in the tool-box?

In the BCP-only days, congregations could follow Holy Communion in a little 'pew' prayer book, turning to the Collect, Epistle and Gospel when the time came, and flicking over a few pages when it came to the exhortations. It was relatively easy to find the words, and to follow the order of the prayers and readings. The congregation could also see the rubrics in the service, although the priest might be doing one or two additional things along the way, and some choral texts and hymns might have been added if they had music. If people were interested (or bored) they might take a look at what else was in the book, and discover all sorts of interesting or surprising things. They might well have had their own copy of the BCP at home, too, and some congregations were encouraged to reflect upon the Collect and readings before coming to the service. They had at least some knowledge of the tools that were being used to craft the service.

In the twenty-first century, many Church of England congregations will be following purpose-made service booklets, or have the words of an entire service projected on to a screen. Texts and rubrics in the booklet will have been chosen by whoever prepared the liturgy, but there is little to indicate to the congregation where things have come from, except by brief mention in the copyright acknowledgements. Furthermore, few people will be able to go home to look up a prayer from one of the *Common Worship* resources, because they won't have, or won't know how to have, access to it. I have met ordinands, for example, who have begun their training without any knowledge of the existence of 'A Service of the Word' from *Common Worship*, or who have rarely had the opportunity to glance at a main volume of *Common Worship*. Apart from the patterns they have become used to in their home parish churches, they have not been aware of a far wider context, nor of the essential structures and principles that lie behind the preparation of liturgy. They simply don't know about the tools of their trade.

How do people come to know what is in the box? This is a key question. Worship leaders need to know what tools are available; where to find them; how to make them work. They need to be well-grounded in this knowledge before they go on to learn how to use them for the best possible outcome, how to prepare, craft and deliver an apt act of worship; how to prepare the soil.

Training and resourcing for the future

If we are to equip the Church to make the best use of our liturgical resources for a worship-filled future, excellent training is crucial – at all stages of ministry, and for all types of ministry that include the leading of worship – both lay and ordained. Training, development and resourcing must be priorities as we look to the years ahead.

An understanding of how worship works, and its relationship to the Church's mission and ministry, grows from a combination of factors, some being God-given gifts and others being skills learnt or acquired.

Ministers need to understand the theology of worship, and learn to be skilled at creating and staging transforming acts of worship. Even though there will be some ministers who do not see their gifts lying in the area of worship, they can still be shown the way that worship can be crafted into a variety of shapes, and they will be able to learn how to combine a set of key components in such a way that the whole thing will really take off. In learning these skills, it is vital for ministers and worship leaders to gain a thorough knowledge of the tools of the trade, and how they work. This sort of knowledge is not something that can be picked up by instinct, or absorbed by osmosis: it is the kind of learning that requires attention, time and experience. It is also best shared with others by the exchange of good practice and ideas.

The establishment of local worship teams, for the preparation and leading of worship, is another key factor for the future, and will reap benefits not only in learning and development, but also as a model of broader liturgical ministry, and of a richer overall contribution to the task. Indeed, it has been good practice for some time, and has much to commend it. In an increasingly mixed economy of lay and ordained ministers (both of whom are manifest in a variety of forms), as well as a declining number of full-time stipendiary clergy, we are all going to have to learn to work more collaboratively.

The necessity for careful attention to the equipping of worship leaders applies right across the traditions, from traditional parishes to Pioneer and Fresh Expressions ministries – the latter, perhaps, requiring the most careful preparation of all, as ministers seek to apply age-old, fundamental principles of worship in new and particularly innovative ways.

IME 1–7

At an official level, a recent element of the Liturgical Commission's work – in partnership with the Ministry Division, and those more widely responsible for Initial Ministerial Education – is the creation of a list of liturgical competencies to be developed within IME 1–7. This may go some way in addressing the need. Perhaps at this point, however, we should pause to reflect upon the growing concerns regarding the small number of specialists teaching worship and liturgy in colleges and courses in England. In the tenth anniversary year of *Common Worship* only three of the eleven theological colleges had a core member of staff with special expertise in this area. Questions of funding for theological education, and concerns over a restricted number of staff required to cover a fairly large number of subject areas between them, are not easily resolved, but since we acknowledge that worship is a core activity of the Church, we must do all that we can to train ministers to the best of their potential.

Enthusing clergy and lay worship leaders to engage in continuing ministerial development of a liturgical kind is a further challenge – not only because of the scarcity of people employed as liturgical educators, but because of the 'opt-in' approach. In addition to this, many ministers – having made a big effort to find out about *Common Worship* at the time of its introduction, now want to move on to other areas of learning.

Central liturgical staff and partner organizations

The Liturgical Commission and the National Worship Development Officer have been very much at the centre of official liturgical development over recent years. With the publication of the study edition of the *Common Worship* ordination services in 2007, and of *Common Worship: Festivals* in 2008, the printed publications of *Common Worship* were complete. The Liturgical Commission recognized that there needed to be a period of time during which the use of *Common Worship* could settle in the Church, so that ministers and congregations might become familiar with the resources available, and put them to best use.

The main thrust of the Liturgical Commission more recently, therefore, has been towards consultancy, training and development in preparing and leading worship; and on building partnerships with organizations sharing the same aims, and with other denominations. The Transforming Worship initiative was launched in 2007, with an accompanying study book, *Worship Changes Lives* and a website.[2] The aim of the initiative is to build skills and gifts among those who prepare and lead worship, based on a theological understanding of the nature of worship and its relation to the mission and work of the Church. This is a huge undertaking, and has been delivered not only by members of the Liturgical Commission, but many partner organizations and, very significantly, by the National

Worship Development Officer, who also planned and co-ordinated much of the delivery.

Many people have expressed concern, therefore, that the post of National Worship Development Officer – the only central liturgical post of this type in the Church of England – has been significantly diminished.

There are a few independent organizations within the church with a concern for liturgical formation and resourcing, but these are run by volunteers, who are very often doing it in their 'spare time' on top of demanding posts in parishes, cathedrals and dioceses. These organizations receive no funding, other than subscriptions from members who share the common concern. The strengthening of partnerships between these willing (and often highly experienced and skilled) people with those responsible for the delivery of training is crucial; but if the resourcing of one of the central purposes of the Church is left to be run on a shoestring and good will, it sends out a confusing signal about the importance of worship, and makes the task all the more difficult.

The wider Church – working together

Since the process of liturgical revision that took place in the second half of the twentieth century, a number of denominations have worked together, producing some common material and drawing material from one another. The Joint Liturgical Group – established in 1963 – enabled some common translations of well-known texts and prayers to be agreed and used by several denominations.

The Liturgical Commission of the Church of England sends representatives to the ecumenical Joint Liturgical Group, and to the writing group for the *Week of Prayer for Christian Unity*. It sends an Anglican observer to the Liturgy Committee of the Catholic Bishops' Conference of England and Wales, to the Worship and Liturgy Resources Group of the Faith and Order Committee of the Methodist Church, and to the Nordic Churches' Liturgy Group. Representatives of the Roman Catholic

Church and Methodist Church also attend the Liturgical Commission as observers.

On a more informal level, Church of England congregations have been drawing on the resources of other places, such as the Taizé and Iona Communities, and have been singing songs gathered from all around the world. In many local parish and chaplaincy contexts, mixed-denomination congregations are getting on and worshipping together. We cannot consider the future of Church of England worship without acknowledging that local ecumenical initiatives and co-operation will be very much part of the picture.

Expansion and review of Common Worship

From time to time people ask if there will be any more of *Common Worship*, and whether a review has been planned. In actual fact, any new textual output by the Liturgical Commission is in response to a request directly from the House of Bishops. As the completion of the *Common Worship* publications came into view, the Liturgical Commission was asked to work on Additional Eucharistic Prayers for use when a substantial proportion of those present are children, some resources for the Admission and Licensing of Readers, and an Additional Weekday Lectionary.

More recently, the Liturgical Commission has been commissioned to revisit the *Common Worship* baptism service. This was among the first of the *Common Worship* services to be produced, and was authorized without the benefit of having been 'road-tested', as were subsequent draft services. On the whole, however, the Commission recognizes that it is time for the focus of attention to change, and that textual work will cease to hold the profile of previous years.

Attitudes to worship – shifting ground

There is no doubt that the rapidly changing culture in Britain over past decades has had an impact on the Church. These social and cultural changes have implications for the Church's worship, as much as they raise crucial mission questions. The final aspect of our liturgical future to be considered here, therefore, is that of the Church's response to some of the social and cultural changes in the way that it worships.

New patterns of church

Sunday, the traditional day of rest and worship, has been filled with lots of alternative attractions; people tend to spread the regular activities of a busy week into seven days, rather than six; and the Church is no longer the privileged institution that it was, automatically commanding respect and authority. People are more likely to question the need to bother with church, than to come out of a sense of duty or habit. This shapes our future.

The outcome of all of this is that many traditional worshipping communities have become smaller. This has not been the case right across the Church, and some types of community – among which are cathedral congregations – have been growing. At the same time, a diverse range of non-traditional worshipping patterns has been developing. Some have identified a better day and time for them to meet than on Sunday; some do not meet in a church building at all; some meet in network groups that fit more conveniently with their lifestyle, rather than in traditional parish communities; some experiment with innovative worshipping styles; and others are shaping new ways of 'being' church, some of which are only beginning to grow into worshipping communities. This diversity of patterns is undoubtedly part of our liturgical future, and we shall need to encourage those with creative imaginations, as we continue into the twenty-first century.

Impatience

Another change in our society is that we look for and expect immediate gratification. We have taken the waiting out of wanting, to use a familiar phrase from a credit card advert (although we may find that, in a more cautious financial climate, waiting has a bit of a renaissance). A text or email goes in an instant, and the reply comes back from halfway around the world within seconds. We are impatient; in a hurry; we want what we want, straight away.

In our impatience for the immediate, we have lost the art and value of anticipation. We don't come to worship in imaginative expectation; we have forgotten how to wait for God.

We may need to relearn how to 'wait'. How to use space, silence and time to prepare the way for an encounter with God. How to approach worship with personal preparation, opening ourselves to the Holy Spirit and allowing ourselves to be taken by surprise by God. And some of us need to learn how to step aside from the activity-driven, deadline-meeting lives that we lead; to put ourselves into the hands of the one who knows eternity.

Consumer mentality

A third example of social change is the way that having so many options available to us has made us very picky and critical. The consumer is king or queen, and what we want counts. We choose exactly what we want, and disregard that which is uninteresting or less than perfect to us. If something doesn't suit us, or does not turn out to be immediately available, then we simply turn away and look somewhere else. This is not only true of our shopping, it is also how we approach our spare-time activities. It is not surprising, therefore, that the mindset comes into play at church, too, and can be characteristic even of regular, faithful worshippers, who have become accustomed to choosing just what they want. The downside of this is that when people come to a service, they might be approaching as consumers, expecting a spiritual kind of entertainment, waiting to be impressed. It is so easy to forget that it is most often in giving ourselves in worship that we receive blessings from God, and that God is going to find it hard to surprise us if we are more interested in looking for something that will please us.

In general, how might the Church respond to the cultural shifting sands that affect our worship? We must not bury our heads in them, that is for certain. We need to engage with our culture and, as a prevailing culture transforms, we have to assess it afresh, using the values of the kingdom of God as a benchmark, sometimes looking for innovative ways of meeting the challenge.

Jesus calls his disciples to be counter-cultural. We find that the world's values are turned upside-down when the poor, the meek, the reviled and the persecuted are the ones who are blessed. Mary's song, *Magnificat*, declares that God has turned everything topsy-turvy: bringing down the powerful from their thrones and lifting up the lowly; filling the hungry with good things and sending the rich away empty. Christians are called to proclaim that there is another way of living, without following the crowd, to declare that God's values are different, disturbing, challenging.

Being counter-cultural in worship means that we can approach an act of worship without demanding to be impressed, amused or entertained. We strive for excellence in every aspect – as far as we are able, of course – but we give of our best that we may glorify God. Perhaps we need to relearn how to focus on God, and give of ourselves in worship, rather than looking first for what it is that we shall get out of it.

When we have the confidence to be different, we will also have the courage not to be unnecessarily complicated, either. We need to give all that we can, but we need not feel inferior because we do not have the same technology or resources as the congregation up the road. There may be only a few gathered, none may be musicians, and the only visual aid might be a single candle flickering in the darkness. However simple our worship, however, when it is heart-felt and Spirit-filled, then we shall be joining the hosts around the heavenly throne at least as much as those who are having a liturgical jamboree.

If we are seeking a counter-cultural approach to worship that resists the demand to impress one another, that is not to deny that an act of worship that will excite one person will leave another's heart quite cold. There is, certainly, a place for diversity in style and tradition. Our background, culture, experience, personality and so on will all affect our response to the liturgical stimuli. I know people who are in ecstasy at a cathedral choral evensong (which ends with an organ voluntary at such volume that their very bones vibrate as they sit in their fifteenth-century stalls), yet who find the loud, rhythmic beat of a worship band and the informality of a praise service not only alien, but shocking. I also know people with precisely the reverse preferences and opinions. Throughout the history of the Church of England, worship has differed from one church to another to a greater or lesser extent. However we do it, let's worship well.

Amen

We have considered the diversity of our liturgical future, and the specific training and formation needs that lie ahead; we have looked towards the continued consolidation of *Common Worship* and imaginative use of the material contained within its broad bounds, and we recognize that as our social and cultural context changes, the Church will have to rise to fresh challenges in the way that it worships, and not be afraid of being distinctive and different. We have been encouraged to 'wait' for God, and to seek God's glory before we concern ourselves with our own satisfaction.

Let us return, now, to where we began – contemplating the rich textures of worship in heaven, where all are gathered around and in the midst of the dazzling presence of the living God.

John's vision in the book of Revelation has a golden thread woven throughout. Amidst the dreamlike – sometimes night-marish – activity, as the vision unfolds there are regular reprises of the scene in which the spotlight falls on the continuous cycle of worship around God's throne. Vivid depictions of sounds, sights, smells, drama and movement. Vibrant colours – precious stones, shining radiance and flashes of light. Rumblings, thundering, smoke, and music. Myriads of myriads and thousands of thousands of creatures singing in full voice (just imagine the volume) ... and silence. There is movement and stillness, passion and wonder. Above all, there is the one who is seated on the throne, upon whom all are focused, and before whom all fall down on their faces in awe.

Fired by the vision of what transforming worship can be, let us nurture imaginative anticipation in the hearts and minds of Christian leaders and worshippers, to be enflamed by the Spirit of God. Our liturgical future depends on it.

Notes

1 Psalm 130.5, *Common Worship: Services and Prayers for the Church of England*, London, Church House Publishing, 2000.
2 <www.transformingworship.org.uk>.

Afterword
David Stancliffe, musician, liturgist, bishop

NICHOLAS PAPADOPULOS

At the heart of South Canonry, the see house of the bishop of Salisbury, stands the kitchen: not, as might be expected in an episcopal residence, the chapel, and not the study. These are both present, of course. During David Stancliffe's occupancy the former was understated and the latter cluttered. Each contained a prominent piece of furniture bearing witness to two of his great passions: the Church's worship, and early music. A stone altar modelled on that to be found at the east end of Portsmouth Cathedral dominated the chapel, and a rectangular, red-painted virginal the study. But the obvious heart and nerve-centre of the house is the kitchen, situated on the central corridor that runs between the administrative office and the bishop's study, spacious, airy, and looking onto the water meadows beyond. From 1993 to 2010 it too was dominated by a piece of furniture – a round table.

Mention David and Sarah Stancliffe to anyone who has worked with them, visited them, or, frequently, encountered them only fleetingly, and the conversation will soon turn to that table. They are famously hospitable. They open their home and their kitchen to all, they welcome all, and while in Salisbury they readily and regularly fed all, ordinands on retreat, the senior staff in the midst of a meeting, headteachers from across the two counties of the diocese. One of Stancliffe's frequent throwaway remarks was that ordinands in training ought to be taught to cook, because it is around tables and over food and wine that fellowship – communion – is truly forged. Hospitality was as much a feature of Stancliffe's chairmanship of the Liturgical Commission as it was of his episcopacy in Salisbury and of his leadership of the cathedral community in Portsmouth. It was not just that drinks were bought and wine served whenever the Commission gathered. It was not just that parties were hosted for retiring staff and distinguished Commission members. It was that the chairman, engaging with the needs of his members, would on arrival at whatever retreat house or conference centre they were using head for the chapel and rearrange the liturgical furniture. The space had to be right; it had to welcome the Commission's members; and, according to the exacting view of the chairman, it had to be ordered adequately for their purpose.

Hospitality is Stancliffe's preferred context for conversation, and conversation, around that round table or any other, is another of his passions. In his book *God's Pattern* he relates how a colleague once asked him, 'Have you never realized that you are the kind of person who does his thinking with other people?' 'As a matter of fact,' he adds, 'I hadn't.'[1] For all the clutter of the study, for all its book-lined shelves and piles of paper, it is the personal exchange of ideas that he relishes. He lives daily with the expectation of new encounters, encounters which will interest him and reveal just a little more of the mystery of the divine to him. This was not always easy for those who worked with him in Portsmouth and Salisbury. Provosts and bishops, after all, are expected to have visions and chart strategies; they are expected to pioneer initiatives, and be proficient micro-managers. Stancliffe's preference was always to hear what the other had to say to him. It was how he learned. It was this preference that accounted for his Lenten habit of going to live in a different part of the diocese and spending time listening to the clergy. However, it was among the members of the Liturgical Commission that he found his ideal conversation partners. Their meetings, characterized by stimulating debate and creative exchange, he would always say were among the most vital, invigorating seminars to form and shape his thought. There was, naturally, a cost to this *modus operandi*. In these meetings as in others his enjoyment of the exploration, of the quest, of the journey, rather than of the destination, or of the discovery, could be frustrating for his colleagues and his staff. The goal of the session, after all, might ultimately be the production and final agreement of a Collect or a eucharistic Preface. Stancliffe's preferred sphere was perpetually the intriguingly provisional. He hated to close off options.

If I appear to have described an artist flitting from one canvas to another and never seeing any work through to completion, then I have been very unfair. The preparation of *Common Worship* – the comprehensive renewal of the liturgy of the Church of England – was a mammoth undertaking. The ambition was huge. It was not just to create an 'Alternative' to the Book of Common Prayer, as the Church had in 1980. It was to create *common* worship for the Church. It was to create an overarching structure that would embrace and support almost every act of worship from a Family Service 'hymn sandwich' to the Easter Liturgy with Baptism and Confirmation, from Morning Prayer on Sundays to the Ordination of Bishops. It was to create liturgy with which all the traditions of the Church could worship with integrity. It was to create a library of resources that could be deployed as place or season demanded. Perhaps remarkably, as has become clear over the decade that this volume celebrates, the undertaking was a success. Those who worked with him have little hesitation in attributing that success to Stancliffe. While he loved the cut and thrust of Commission meetings and thrived on their broad-brush deliberations (*which* theology of atonement should this seasonal penitential rite plead; *which* element of the Gelasian Sacramentary should this ordination prayer reflect?) he would also work minutely on draft texts, correcting, amending and re-submitting them late into the night. And for a bishop who was not a natural in the world of synodical processes he proved himself adept at navigating them, piloting *Common Worship* adroitly through its various Byzantine stages.

Salisbury's Ordained Local Ministry Scheme owed its beginning to a conversation Stancliffe once had with a group of

Wiltshire churchwardens. The vicar of their several villages had retired. When, they wanted their bishop to tell them, would they get another? 'As soon as you like,' he replied. Astounded, they looked at him expectantly. 'Just tell me which of you I should ordain,' he added. The role of the bishop, he believed, was to hand on the responsibility which had been handed to him, the responsibility for proclaiming the Gospel afresh and for nurturing the common life of Christ's body; the role of the bishop (indeed the role of any of the baptized) was never to hog that responsibility and lord it over others. When inducting new clergy into posts in the diocese he would often remind them that the words 'Receive this cure of souls, which is both yours and mine' did not mean 'Over to you now.' It meant an invitation to a partnership. He expected similar relationships with members of the Liturgical Commission. Their role was not to defer to him. He looked for robust debate in committee, and insisted on handing over responsibility for different areas of *Common Worship* to different members. They were entrusted with preparing drafts in those areas, and although they would be expected to defend their work on the floor of the Commission it would never occur to Stancliffe to undermine their authority or subvert their position.

What I have described is a fourfold pattern. Engagement with people (frequently offering them hospitality); attentiveness to what interests them (and to what they want to communicate); transformation of the situation (often through the bringing to bear of personal gifts to effect that transformation); and the handing on of the responsibility (with an expectation that others will in turn engage, attend and transform). Anyone who has heard Stancliffe preach or who has read his words will recognize this pattern: for him, it is God's pattern. It is played out above all in Luke's account of the appearance to the disciples of Christ on the road to Emmaus.[2] The unrecognized stranger comes alongside the dejected pair and engages with them: 'What are you discussing with each other while you walk along?' Then, having listened to them, he attends to their need of answers: 'Was it not necessary that the Messiah should suffer these things . . . ?' Then, having attended to them, he acts to transform the situation: 'When he was at the table with them, he took bread, blessed and broke it, and gave it to them. Then their eyes were opened, and they recognized him . . .'. Then, having transformed the situation, he hands them the task of acting on it: 'That same hour they got up and returned to Jerusalem . . .'. 'God in Christ does three things for us,' Stancliffe would conclude on Maundy Thursday, at clergy conferences, and in pre-ordination charges (engagement and attentiveness being sometimes rolled into one), 'he shares our life; then he changes it; then he hands us the responsibility of bearing him to others.'

It is this pattern that Stancliffe sought to model in his episcopal ministry, and it is this pattern which is perhaps his most significant contribution to *Common Worship*. A huge number of texts and resources are included in the library; they permit a vast array of seasonal and local adaptations of the liturgy; but what remains constant is the recommended pattern (or structure) which prefaces each rite. His insistence on the pattern was not fussiness or precision for the sake of performance. His insistence on the pattern was rooted in his conviction that the pattern is God's and that it is effective both for the world's transformation and for our redemption. Get the pattern right, he believed, and what words you use for the Confession or for the Intercessions or for the Post-Communion Prayer does not matter. Get the pattern right, and the liturgy will engage worshippers, attend to them, transform them and send them out with a mission to accomplish. Get the pattern right, and through the liturgy God will engage, attend, transform and send. Get the pattern – God's pattern – right and in our common worship as in our common life God's transforming work will be done.

Notes

1 David Stancliffe, *God's Pattern*, London, SPCK, 2003, p. xii.
2 Luke 24.13–35.